THE ENERGY PRINCIPLES

Manifest Your Goals of Success, Money, Love and Health

By MARIE DIAMOND

Feng Shui Master

and Master Teacher in the

Global Phenomena "The Secret"

Copyright and Published by Marie Diamond Publishing

www.MarieDiamond.com

Published in the USA

By Marie Diamond Publishing

Office@mariediamond.com

www.MarieDiamond.com

www.MarieDiamond.com

ISBN 978-1-7377357-2-4

Dedication and Gratitude

I dedicate this book to all the teachers, authors, speakers, and students on the path of Transformation that walked before me on this planet and who brought Transformation to Humanity.

I hope this book will help you to make positive changes in your life and that it makes an impactful contribution towards the Enlightenment of Humanity.

I am grateful to my family, my students, and my teachers. I am especially grateful for my son ACE for creating the cover of my book, and to my Diamond Team.

With Love,

Marie Diamond

www.MarieDiamond.com

Diamond Energy Principles

CONTENTS

Introduction

You are the center of your transformation in your Universe. You are the creator of your own personal reality show. Most reality shows explore topics such as: conflicts, financial problems, loneliness, fighting, cursing, cheating, and other negative human behavior. If this reflects your current personal reality show, you are at the right place: it is time for transformation.

Just imagine the millions of viewers watching your reality TV show right now. Would you like to show them the above negative experiences, or harmony, success, and happiness instead?

On the TV channels, unfortunately, the reality of pain and suffering is still selling, but is this what you wish to have in your life? You are the responsible creator of your own TV show: you are the producer, the director and the actor. You have the power to make the decisions to transform your life *right now*.

May this book support you in having the best-rated, most successful and inspirational TV show in the Universe.

Every day, I hear stories from people that used the Diamond Energy Principles as explained in this book to manifest a better life for themselves, their families and friends. My wish for you is that this book will be your guide to a fast, effortless, and easy transformation in your life.

I hope this book will receive an honorable place in your life. Place it in your personal success direction in your living room, bedroom or office so that you can activate it with success. Or, you can put it in the Southwest direction of your bedroom, living room or office so that I can, from a distance, support you with your transformation.

You will see that sometimes resistance will come up while reading this book. This doesn't necessarily have to be a negative thing! It simply means that you need to let go of something old and that something better wants to emerge into your life. Resistance is an indication that you are on the right track, that you want to become more successful and happier. Your ego has kept you occupied for far too long. It has kept you in fear and imprisoned you in the clusters of your own limitations. Whenever you feel resistance in changing something in your life or your environment, it is an indication that when you will change, you will experience more freedom and happiness.

So, why not just try it out? I always suggest making the change and seeing if you feel a shift within 9 days. See if you feel better and if you do, keep the new change. If you still feel uncomfortable, wait a few more days or you can change again. You are free to change your life back to what it was. Remember, you are the decision maker.

Most people will say that their family and friends will comment on noticing "something different" about them. If they do, you are on the right path towards transforming your life.

This book will support you, step by step, to create lasting transformation. Try to practice one thing from every chapter you read. You do not have to do it all at once. Even just one little change can start shifting the energy. That is why after each chapter, you will find space to journal. This is space in the book where you can journal about what insights you received in the chapter you just read.

After doing these simple steps, start applying the rest of this book to your life and environment. It will be an amazing journey of transformation.

All My Love to All of You.
Marie Diamond
www.*MarieDiamond.com*

First Part:
General Diamond Energy Principles

Chapter 1:
The Three Aspects of the Law of Attraction.

When I met my Grandmaster in Feng Shui, Master Yap, in 1994, he shared that there are three aspects of the Law of Attraction and all three have an equal amount of impact on your life. The three aspects are: 33% of Heaven Luck, 33% of Human Luck and 33% of Earth Luck.

These three aspects of your manifestation process will help you understand how the Law of Attraction may not have always created the results you wanted in the past.

Most people in countries that have daily food, healthy water, education, and healthcare have already 20% of their Heaven Luck fulfilled. The fact that you are reading this book and are interested in improving yourself tells me that you are working to have positive thoughts, feelings, and actions in your life. Let's say you already have 20% Human Luck fulfilled.

But Transformation is also at work in your environment. That is the area where you can easily gain percentages, as it is the easiest way to change. When you have about 20% of your Earth Luck in place, the Law of Attraction works easily and effortlessly, and things manifest magically. You will experience that you are in a flow of being at the right place at the right time and meeting the right people.

Heaven Luck

Before your Soul came to Earth, I believe it made decisions about what lessons it wished to learn and what experiences it wished to have. Your Heaven luck is responsible for 33% of your Law of Attraction. Connecting with your Soul while meditating, praying, and contemplating will help you to change your Heaven Luck and improve it.

Heaven Luck was already at work when you were born. You, as a Soul, attracted your parents, your country, and your life conditions so you could learn some valuable life experiences called Soul lessons.

Your Soul made conscious choices like about your parents and the circumstances you grew up in. Your Soul didn't make the choices based on comfort but based on spiritual growth. Or, maybe you believe that God/the Universe has chosen them for you.

Some would call this your destiny, your faith or your karma. The ones who believe in previous life experiences would say you attracted this because of your thoughts, feelings, and actions from a previous life experience.

So, your destiny influences 1/3 of your life's luck.

You live on a planet where your Free Will is the highest asset. It's good to know you can decide how to evolve your life.

Can you change your Heaven Luck?

Who and where you are born, the parents you have, the culture and country you start in, will keep influencing you to a certain degree. The talents you are born with will always be there for you to use.

But elders in many religious or belief systems tell us that we can change our destiny.

My Feng Shui Grandmaster Yap told me specifically that: "By changing your Earth Luck (changing your location on this planet) your Human Luck will change, and ultimately, so will your Heaven Luck."

We know today that, in this modern world, you can change a large part of your Heaven Luck. You can change your gender, you can marry into another culture and immigrate to another country. Even through adoption you can change families. But all of the basic parts of your destiny will keep influencing you in some way.

Some spiritual teachings even go further. They say that every human being born on this planet had several life experiences before this one. The past life experiences will reflect in the life circumstances you were born into and the challenges and talents that you express in this life.

Astrology is a semi - science that can help you understand your destiny. But I believe it is telling us only possibilities, not final outcomes. I remember when I connected with a very famous Vedic astrologer. He told me that my destiny was to be a mother, a modern prophet, a teacher, or someone bringing forward interior design. Well, I am a mother of three children, teach Universal Laws and am a Feng Shui Master. I am apparently fulfilling my destiny but how I am doing it, is up to me.

Heaven Luck involves your religious beliefs (whatever beliefs you may have) and your spiritual practice (going to church, meditating, studying with spiritual leaders, and meditative practices like Yoga and Qigong). I believe having a daily religious or spiritual practice will increase your Heaven Luck.

Human Luck

The second aspect of the Law of Attraction is called Human Luck. It is the part that most self-help authors and speakers write or teach about. Most people create the reality around them through their thoughts, feelings, and actions.

Well, creating the right human luck in your life is to show up with the right thoughts, right feelings and doing the right things in your life. Even if the day doesn't look so bright, you still show up for yourself and others. As a teacher showing up to teach your students, as a salesperson showing up to sell, as a business owner showing up to do business with your clients and as a stay-at-home mom, showing up to take care of your children and your family.

Living your life with the right mindset, a grateful and loving heart and an action plan is using your Human Luck to its full potential. In the reality show of your life, no one is producing and directing it but YOU. You need to give yourself the directions in your mind and heart and you need to be the one doing the steps and calling "Action" and "Cut" when you feel you get the scene right. If you don't get the right scene, you start all over again, if necessary, hundreds of times.

Your Human Luck is creating 33% of your Transformation. It is something you can work on. It takes discipline and the right tools and techniques.

The movie and best seller "The Secret", where I am one of the featured Master Teachers, has been a great wake up call for people to change their thoughts, feelings and actions in a more positive way. The whole self-help movement is a great support in changing your Human Luck.

Once you start your Transformation process, you start to quickly wake up and you find that many millions are waking up with you. The self-improvement industry with all the self-help books and videos and CDs are booming, and movies like "The Secret" are helping people to attain at least 20% or more of their Human Luck.

But let's face it, it takes time to change your thoughts from negative to positive. It takes time to let go of your emotional programs and it takes discipline and courage to make your dreams come true. Without action, nothing happens.

It is a constant daily exercise to love yourself and to stop the negative voices in your head that brings you doubt and lets you live in fear. You need to practice attaining Human Luck and honestly you will need your whole life to keep this muscle of positive energy in shape.

Every transformational book that you can read, every Transformational teacher that you can listen to, will say the practice gets easier with time.

You have a Personality or Ego, which has a task to keep interfering with your mindset and stop your Soul from accessing your Universal Greatness.

It is here that the Ego comes into play and creates friction and resistance for you. But through this game of resisting your greatness and transforming your fears and doubts, you are shaping yourself and evolving to become the Master of your life.

Be grateful for the resistance and negative thoughts and feelings. They help you to transform your life. My attitude toward my Ego is to handle it as a child with an attitude. When it starts nagging me with self-pity and doubt and fear, I say: It is all right. Everything will be alright. I hug it with love, I hold it in my loving heart, but I don't let it run my life and dictate the rest of my day. Fear and doubt will keep you away from the freedom of being who you are.

When you hit rock bottom in your misery, then you start asking questions: Why is this happening to me? Whose fault is this that I feel bad. Why is all this bad luck happening to me? Why did I attract this abusive partner? Why did I lose my job? Why am I without money? Why can I not find a loving partner?

Of course, when you are not consciously awake, you try to blame it first on everything outside of yourself: your partner, your children, your boss, your parents, your friends, your leaders, your country and, finally, if you can't find anybody else, God. You continue attracting exactly what you have been focusing on, because blame doubles the effect: more abuse, more bad luck, more lack of money and more loneliness.

Then the light bulb finally goes on and the egg of misery cracks open, Hallelujah.... "Perhaps I created this myself? Blaming someone else is not the cause of my problem. Who is the one in the center of all my problems? Me? What if I start looking at myself? And take responsibility for my own thoughts, feelings, and actions.

The awakening process starts happening by a conversation, a book, a movie, talking with a friend, a church sermon, an AA meeting, watching "The Secret" or reading this book.

Then you become aware: You are the Creator of your own life. God/The Universe is in you. You are responsible for your own life. You are the Divine within. You need to take responsibility.

Are you Ready to attract a Better Life?

Let's be honest, in the beginning you get it, but you turn away from it immediately. It's too simple or it's too hard. Even if you get it, it is still hard to start living with these new insights. I am sure you have attended many workshops and read books that give you all great tools about how to turn your life around. You get an "Aha!" moment, but what about now?

You promise to change but before you know it, life has taken over and your "Aha!" moment is gone. Why could you not continue with your Transformation?

Over the years of personal research and studying, I found that it is not because you changed your thoughts, feelings and actions, that you integrated the change into your life.

You need to understand that what is around you as your environment influences you also for 33%.

And when your environment is not supporting your inner changes, the changed attitude is not rooted in your current reality.

Many self-help workshops give you a high moment. You believe you can change and definitely you can. Unfortunately, you will spend a weekend or a retreat with a wonderful teacher, you will study fabulous knowledge, and will share it with a like-minded community and you totally believe: "Now I got it. Now my life will change."

But after this inspiring time, you go back to your home. You go back to the same environment before the weekend. And your environment is still reflecting your old reality and before you know it, you are falling back into your old routine even if you don't want to. You fall back asleep or the awakening slows down.

In this book, you will receive actions to change your Human Luck, but you will also receive steps to change the next important part of your Law of Attraction.

Earth Luck

Your Environment is responsible for 33% of your Law of Attraction. It is a part of Transformation that most people are ignorant about. The Chinese Feng Shui Masters have for more than 4,000 years been aware of that not only "Location is everything", but that how the building is set up in the landscape and what is in the location is as important.

Your home is the Soundboard of God/the Universe. It is where the Universal energy can manifest itself. You are God/Universe within you, and you are God/Universe around you.

Perhaps you don't see the oneness between you and the outside world, but the quantum field connects everything with each other.

As Einstein already shared: "Everything is Energy". Even the vastest forms are made out of energy. Energy is a living principle. As you are breathing in the energy of Life, so is your home. Every time you open the doors and the windows toward the outside world, your home is breathing in the Universal Life Force.

Because it is so much more vast than your own physical body, you may not experience that it has its own energy. Your home has a life of its own.

Your home is the exterior layer between your inner God experience and the outer God experience. It is the inbox and outbox of your messages to God/Universe.

When your home is in total chaos, you cannot expect that your messages are going to find their way to the outside world. Your home is the first layer of the outside world. If you block this energy, the manifestation of your dreams cannot happen. You can't expect the gifts of God/Universe to arrive into your life when your home is closed up to receive them.

How your location is set up, is 33% of the impact on your Success, Abundance, Health, Relations and Wisdom. The best news is that changing your environment is an easy thing to do. It does not take discipline. It just takes knowledge and a short-term action plan.

In this book, you will receive many practical Energy and Feng Shui steps to improve your Success, Health, Relationship and Wisdom.

Most Transformational teachings share that the God/Universe is within you. And I do acknowledge this completely, but they are missing a very important aspect: The God/Universe is also around you.

As you are in oneness with the field that you live and work in, what is around you influences you as much as what is within you. These two directions inside out and outside in, are complementary to each other.

You will learn the basic steps of how you can align within and around you in total alignment. These are basic steps that you can practice wherever you are living or working.

You will find them in this book by learning the Diamond Energy principles. When you use these steps, you will always be in perfect harmony with the God/Universe around you and so you will manifest a more harmonious and happy energy within you.

Can You Change your Earth Luck?

You can change your Earth Luck and it is easy. Improving your home is easier than changing your thoughts, feelings and actions. Changing your bed, changing pictures, changing the flow, can all be done in a couple of hours. Changing your destiny and changing your thoughts and feelings, can take many years of practice. But changing your environment can affect you within minutes and create change within days and weeks. In this Book, I will share with you 24 Diamond Energy Principles that will increase the results of your Law of Attraction.

The Diamond Energy Journal

Once you've become familiar with the Diamond Energy Principles, commit to your own Diamond Energy Journey with my book "The Diamond Energy Journal".

Filled with thoughtful journal prompts, a range of engaging tasks and Feng Shui tips, you'll learn how to manifest the live of your dreams. Available on www.MarieDiamond.com or on Amazon.

Chapter 2: Inner and Outer Energy.

You Are the Center of the Universe

Remember it always starts with the star in the TV show and that is you. You need to prepare yourself every day to show up in the Universe. Bring yourself into the right vibration by focusing on your Inner Light and stimulating your Inner Power.

Connect with the loving and supporting energy that you have already attracted and take a moment to be grateful. Then, let go of all the negative experiences, thoughts and feelings, and let go of the worst of all: your own limiting beliefs and programs.

You need to shine your Inner Light, you need to be protected by the right energy, you need to surround yourself with wonderful friends and you need to stay humble and above your Ego.

When I speak about God/Universe, I want to acknowledge that people have many names for the creative force that created you, your world, the planets, and the entire galaxy.

This book is written with total respect for your ancient rites, religions, and cultures. No matter how your connection with God/Universe is expressed, you will see that this book will help you become a better human being with more devotion or a stronger connection with God/ Universe.

You Are the Universe Within You

Everything is one, as the enlightened masters, mystics in many religions and shamans worldwide experienced in their inner awareness.

There is no limit between the Universe outside of you and the Universe inside of you. Oneness is experiencing that everything you are is within you and also created outside of you and vice versa. Living in this Oneness field is called self-realization or enlightenment.

So, why keep looking outside of yourself any longer and waiting for someone to help rescue you? Start by rescuing yourself. In order to do this, I started a daily spiritual exercise called the "Tubes of Light Meditation" that my Spiritual Master shared with me when I was seven years old. It will be a great help for you in your process of change. In the free Marie Diamond app (for iPhones and smartphones), you can listen to an audio of me sharing this meditation.

Be Open for Support in Your Transformation

I know you are the center of the Universe, but you don't have to be alone in your reality show. Open up to help and support, and be sure to let others know you are creating another reality.

Find a Diamond Energy partner: someone that loves self-improvement. You don't want the help of someone who is critical of your transformational process.

Look for the one who wants to read this book with you, or you can buy two books and share it with a friend so that you go through the steps together.

When you download the free Marie Diamond app in the App store or Google Play, you will receive daily Energy messages to support you in your Diamond Energy Journey.

How to Make the Most Out of This Book

Life is an ongoing changing flow of energy. Also, when you are in a downward spiral, you need to shift the flow upwards.

Many studies acknowledge that you need a minimum of 21 to 30 days of constant work on yourself to start seeing results. Well, let this book be your personal mentor on the road to your transformation.

Books are friends that encourage you and motivational authors are mentors that have walked the path before you.

What Do You Need to Do?

- Take time in your day to read one chapter.
- Write down your insights and action steps in the Energy Journal section after each chapter.
- Take one action step within 24 hours to anchor any inspirational thoughts you receive from reading each chapter.
- Share you action step with at least with one person, either on social media, in an email or in a conversation.
- Be grateful every day for the inspiration and that the book that came into your life.

You will see the flow of energy start to shift within 9 days.

The secret to success is to keep reading this book after the first change is occurring. The first sign of change is just the first drop of water coming out of the source. You need a minimum of 21 to 30 days to see a major energy shift in your life.

Transformation is Around You.

Do you remember how you felt when you first moved into your new home or apartment and you positioned all your furniture, painted the walls, placed all the ornaments and hung the paintings?

You probably felt like a great new start was happening in your life. Perhaps, after a while you felt the need to change the design of your home again. You have no idea why, but you just felt your environment was not connecting with you anymore. Even if you couldn't explain what it was, you knew something had shifted.

Human beings have always looked for shelter against the dangers of life. The early human beings looked for shelter in natural places, like caves, because they didn't know how to build houses. But even in these natural places, they added art and color to their shelter because it made them feel safer.

The Influence of Your Home on Your Brainwaves.

In 2005, I introduced a learning course on Diamond Feng Shui to Learning Strategies. In it, I claim that the Universe around you is affecting the state of your mind. When you have a harmonious environment, brainwaves change from Beta to Alpha in a few seconds.

Because I see energy in people's aura fields, chakras, and their environment since childhood, I said to Dr. Paul Scheele, the founder of Learning Strategies and one of the geniuses of the mind: "The Universe around us has an immediate and instant impact on your brainwaves."

Pete Bissonette, CEO of Learning Strategies, told his business partner, Paul Scheele: "You can't walk into a room and have your brain waves change automatically just because somebody did Feng Shui on the room."

The scientist in Paul said, "Let's test it." So, they hooked up a human test subject to a portable EEG machine that was used to measure brain waves.

The subject didn't know what was to be expected. They brought her into a room with no Feng Shui activations or cures. Then they brought her into a room where the principles of Diamond Feng Shui had been applied.

The Beta waves began changing within seconds. The brain began accessing Alpha waves. By simply being in a room with good Feng Shui, the brain began performing at different levels.

The Impact of the Energy of Your Home on Your Life

The science of the mind has known for years that deep-seated, far-reaching benefits come from being in the Alpha state of mind.

This is also the flow state where athletes break world records, actors bring audiences to tears, scientists have their 'Eureka!' moments, and people make visionary decisions.

And now by making simple changes in your home or office, you can bring your mind into the Alpha state where you can literally direct good fortune into your life.

Your Environment is Energy

In the book, 'The Answer", John Assaraf, explains brilliantly how everything is Energy and how, through the Law of Resonance, everything resonates with each other.

From a quantum physics perspective, you and your environment exist together in space. You are both conscious and unconscious awareness. The ratio of unconscious to conscious is 83% - 17% and the unconscious brain process is amazingly much faster than your conscious brain process.

You could say that your unconscious brain process reacts with the speed of light. Your consciousness knows the past and future, but your unconsciousness is living in the now.

Your environment is totally unconscious, and it reacts with the same speed as your unconscious brain process and lives in the now, 24 hours a day.

I share with people that whatever is in the Universe around you is always working, and through the Law of Resonance, it is always influencing your brainwaves. This constant process will affect your thoughts, your feelings and your body.

I believe that the missing link of the Law of Attraction is how your environment affects your thinking.

When asked when things went bad in their business, people answer the following: *"After I moved or within one year of moving into this building."*

When asked when things went wrong in their romance: *"After redoing the interior of my home."*

When asked when their health became worse: *"After they changed the roof and added another part of the home."*

The Link Between Your Home and Your Good Luck

Well, for more than 4,000 years, the Chinese Feng Shui Masters have been aware of this missing link. Even the queens and kings believed it: King Louis XIV of France and Peter I from Russia are believed to have brought Feng Shui Masters into their palaces. Multinational corporations like Virgin, Body Shop, British Airways, BP-Amoco, and

Disney, to just name a few, are looking into this new approach for creating better wellbeing and more abundance for their employees and customers.

Impact the Universe Around You and You Will Impact the Universe Within You

You will learn in this book the Earth Luck steps that will support you in changing your life. I call them the 24 Diamond Energy Principles and they work to increase the results of your Law of Attraction by 33.3%. They are Universal principles to support your transformation. They work for everyone, everywhere.

Your Energy Journal

At the end of each chapter, you'll find a blank page for you to write down your thoughts, feelings and action plans inspired by what you've read. This is a judgement-free space, so honor yourself by writing down your absolute truth.

Part Two:
THE 24 DIAMOND ENERGY PRINCIPLES

Introduction

Since studying and practicing the Law of Attraction for more than 50 years, I understood that there are 24 Diamond Energy Principles, which work for everyone, everywhere, every time and in everything. The 24 principles are divided into six Success Energy principles, six Health Energy principles, six Relationship Energy principles, and six Wisdom Energy principles.

You can activate these principles in yourself and in the world around you, so that you can effortlessly increase the results of the Law of Attraction in your life.

Each principle will be viewed from the Universe within you and from the Universe around you. You will start to understand how strong each principle is working in your life and how you can, through easy tools and colors, manifest them.

Masters of Transformation express these 24 principles as much as they can in their daily life. Remember, Transformational leaders are not always perfect, but they try to live the most spiritual lives in their human experience, and they share transformational tools, skills and wisdom with the rest of humanity.

Knowing what principals to focus on to reach the highest level of Success, Health, Relationships and Wisdom, will make it easier for you to transform your life and to become a Transformational Leader in your community. The 24 principles will give you a road map about what you still need to work on to master your Transformational process in this lifetime.

My vision and destiny on this planet is to enlighten more than 500 million people using these 24 Diamond Energy Principles to support them. In the last 30 years, I've already impacted millions of people in more than 190 countries by appearing in "The Secret" and working with publishers like Learning Strategies and Mind Valley. I am so grateful that people worldwide have experienced positive changes in their lives.

Of course, I have already had some moments of drama, grief and pain, but I turned them around as I learned to transform my life. Any difference you make in yourself and in your family and community is part of creating a Transformational World.

By transforming your Success, your Health, your Relationships and your Wisdom in the best way you can, you will improve not only yourself but the people living around you. That is the ultimate goal: making yourself happy and to make others happy around you. Mastering Transformation is living 24 hours a day in a perfect alignment with the Universe.

These 24 Diamond Energy principles are already in your awareness, but you need to awaken their potential. By reading this book and practicing, you will strengthen what is already present within you. Some of the principles will feel very natural to you whilst others may feel a little harder to focus on.

In my Inner Diamond Meditation Program, I support you to activate these Diamond Energy Principles with meditation techniques. For more information join www.MarieDiamond.com.

The 24 Diamond Energy principles are divided into 12 male – active Energy principles (Yang) and 12 female – passive Energy principles (Yin). They are brought together as 12 yin yang symbols. So, the yang/male principles are projecting energy frequencies and the yin/female principles are receiving energy frequencies. Whatever direction you start with, you will always attract the complimentary.

Some teachings will tell you to start with sending information out to the Universe. Tell the Universe what you really want to attract by sharing your goals, making a vision board, affirming out loud what you wish to manifest, praying and meditating.

These are practices that are using the spirit and the mind to create Transformational changes. The energy will follow the information and manifest into form. Information is going from the Universe within you towards the Universe around you to create your reality.

Other teachings will share with you how the energy can be created or tapped into. You can do this with practices like Feng Shui, Qigong, and yoga. These are practices that are using the flow of energy in the body and in the environment to create transformational shifts in your mind and spirit.

Energy is going from the Universe around you towards the Universe within you to create your reality.

Is one way better than the other? Not necessarily, but it's best to use both at the same time. In this book I will guide you in using both at the same time to create more results with your Law of Attraction.

Overview of the 24 Diamond Energy Principles

You can activate them within yourself and your environment.

12 Male Energy Principles	12 Female Energy Principles
Power	Empowerment
Wisdom	Compassion
Love	Tenderness
Healing	Truth
Purity	Transparency
Balance	Passion
Forgiveness	Release
Clarity	Focus
Joy	Celebration
Abundance	Magnificence
Peace	Collaboration
Transformation	Faith

Four Pillars of the 24 Diamond Energy Principles

You can also divide the 24 Diamond Energy principles into four pillars:

1/ Your Success and Abundance
2/ Your Health and Wellbeing
3/ Your Relationships
4/ Your Wisdom and Inspiration

1/ Diamond Energy Principles for Success and Abundance

To attract more success, career and money, you need to master the following six principles:

Power (Royal blue)	Empowerment (Cobalt blue)
Abundance (Gold)	Magnificence (Silver)
Joy (Peach)	Celebration (Orange)

When you transform your Success, you become a more powerful, joyful person that empowers others and who focuses more on magnifying positive energy in the world and celebrates success.

2/ Diamond Energy Principles for Health and Wellbeing

To attract more physical, emotional, mental and spiritual health, you need to master these six principles:

Healing (Emerald green)	Truth (Citrus green)
Purity (White)	Transparency (Ivory white)
Forgiveness (Violet)	Release (Lilac)

When you transform your Health, you become a more healing and forgiving person that is more honest with themselves and others, who acts with more transparency and releases the blockages from the past.

3/ Diamond Energy Principles for Relationships

To attract positive personal and professional relationships in your life, you need to master the following six principles:

Love (Rose)	Tenderness (Pink)
Balance (Ruby red)	Passion (Cherry red)
Peace (Magenta)	Collaboration (Fuchsia)

When you transform your Relationships, you become a more loving and peaceful person who expresses more tenderness with others, someone who is more passionate in living their dreams and collaborates easily with others.

4/ Diamond Energy Principles for Wisdom

To attract more inner wisdom, knowledge, education and connection with God/Universe, you need to master the following six principles:

Wisdom (Yellow)	Compassion (Saffron yellow)
Clarity (Aqua)	Focus (Iris blue)
Transformation (Opal)	Faith (Diamond)

When you transform your Wisdom, you become a wiser person that becomes more compassionate towards other people's beliefs and cultures, has an open focus on a positive future, and is faithful to their vision, purpose, and goals.

In the following chapters, I will explain each Diamond Energy Principle and how it works in the Universe within you, and around you. I will give you Feng Shui tips to activate it in your environment. Also, I will share with you the colors connected with the Diamond Energy Principles and how to use them.

A. Energize your Success

To help enhance your success, career and money, there are six Diamond Energy Principles that you can activate. These principles are:

- Power
- Empowerment
- Abundance
- Magnificence
- Joy
- Celebration

You will encounter details about these principles in the next chapter.

The Diamond Energy Principle of Power

"I Am Power in All I Am and in All I Do"

1/ The Diamond Energy Principle of Power

Power is the first Diamond Energy Principle and activates your Success. You will learn how to activate this within you and in the space around you, so you can attract 33% more success and abundance.

a/ Your Inner Activation of Power

You are powerful. The word "power" for many people is a contaminated word and I would love to change this. "Power" as a word has always been connected with the idea of an Almighty God or Person.

Some cultures connect with the power of their God(s). It seems like only God or the Gods and the people ruling in their name, have been able to experience the true Power of the Universe. Power does seem to hold a level of respect or dignity in it, but the moment power is connected with human beings, we are less sure that it can exist without abuse.

Well, there are two different ways of expressing power: power from the soul or power of the ego. I would like to give you some values connected with the two different approaches.

When You Use the Power of Your Soul:

- You are respectful towards others, your environment, and the planet
- You think inclusively and work to create bridges between people, cultures, races, and countries
- You honor the Laws of the Universe expressed in religion, philosophies, and spiritual practices
- You connect with a higher purpose
- You promote confidence, courage and empowerment
- You listen to solutions that are given to you by your intuition

When You Use the Power of Your Ego:

- You are indifferent, abusive, or harmful to others, your environment and the planet
- You think exclusively and work to create divisions between people, cultures, races and countries
- You are indifferent to the Laws of the Universe expressed in religion, philosophies and spiritual practices
- You connect with greed, self-interest, chaos and anarchy
- You promote anger, fear and violence
- You are controlling, see yourself as the only salvation to the problem, and are incapable of listening to others

Most people are living their lives from the power of the ego and are surprised when they attract exactly the same back. Living as a Master of Transformation, you need to connect with the power of your soul. Spiritual or religious practices are very important because it reminds you to use the power of your soul.

In ancient cultures and religions, it was important to go to a place to connect with the power of God at least once a week. This power is always expressed by a triangle with the top up. That is why priests wore hats in a cone or triangle form. The triangle down is connected with the ego.

Even temples and churches have domes and towers showing the connection with the power of God and the Soul. Even the wizards or magicians climbed up to the top of the highest tower in the castle of the king to connect with the higher levels of wisdom, in order to manifest the magical formulas.

Now we live in a time where we need to stop thinking that the power of the soul only belongs to the priests and shamans. You have always had access to the inner power of your soul and it's time to connect with it in order to create Transformation in your Life.

Diamond Energy Exercise

Take time to relax and close your eyes. Connect within by breathing consciously in and out. Then visualize yourself in a beautiful space in nature where you feel in complete harmony and peace. Imagine there is a quantum rainbow in the sky with 24 colors. You connect in with the royal blue aspect of this rainbow and fill your body with this color. From your head to your feet, you are filled with the royal blue energy of the Universe.

As you breathe in, you fill yourself with power and as you breathe out you are letting go of every thought, feeling and past action that has limited your inner power. After this, you can connect with a situation, a goal or a relationship where you wish to have more power and visualize the color royal blue around and in it, until you feel the power completely

Say the following affirmation: ***"I Am Power in All I Am and in All I Do."*** Focus again on the beautiful space around you in your visualization and open your eyes.

b/ The Diamond Energy Color of Power

The color of power that can help you attract a powerful position in your life and career is royal blue. The name already lets you know that you are royal. Royal comes from the French: "Royal", pertaining to the king. It is also connected with the Egyptian word for the sun god, "Ra or Re".

Royal means that you are the king or queen of all. You are the royalty of everything in your life. And, indeed, when you connect with the Power of the Universe within you, you are the creator; the one who manifests everything.

You will see that this royal blue color has been used by many French kings, like Louis XIV, to express that they were the representatives of God on Earth. In fact, Louis XIV was called the "Roi Soleil" meaning the Sun King. You sometimes wonder how much they knew consciously about all this information.

How can you use this Color Royal Blue?

- Place a royal blue item in the North area of your office, in the North corner of your bedroom and living room
- Wear a royal blue dress or tie matching your suit for a job interview or an important business meeting

c/ Your Feng Shui Activation of Power

Your home is the unconscious expression of yourself. When I enter a home or office, I always look for signs to see if people feel powerful. As you are the universe within, you need to be in power in your life. When you are not in power, you are not attracting what you really desire. Instead you will stay connected with a poor consciousness and will feel vulnerable and weak. You will feel that you are the victim of your reality instead of being the master of your life.

European kings and queens, the emperors of China, and all political leaders have one thing in common: they sought a long and powerful government. They wanted to be the masters of their countries.

Your life is like a country. Your wish is to be the master of yourself and to make your dreams come true. What can you change to become the master in your Universe? Here are your first steps.

Step 1: Sit or Sleep as a King or a Queen

Do you see the gifts of the Universe as they come to you or do you sit with your back to them? At your home or workspace, you always need to see who enters, whether from your couch, dining table or desk. Make sure you sit in such a way that you can see the incoming energy.

The Universe comes through the door and not through the windows. So, facing a window and having your back towards the door is not efficient. The Universe walks in when you walk in.

I remember doing a Feng Shui consultation in the office of Jack Canfield, best-selling author of "Chicken Soup of the Soul" and "The Success Principles", and one of the Master Teachers of "The Secret" at his ranch in Santa Barbara. I knocked on his door and when I entered, his back was facing the door and he had to turn around to see me. We had a conversation and I asked him how things were in his business since he placed his office like this.

Well, he told me: "I love looking outside and seeing nature." I said to him: "Jack, you are not here to watch nature, you are here to create a difference through your work." So, I asked him a few simple questions: Have you lately felt that people are not recognizing your true value? Have you felt that deals were going on behind your back that you are not a part of?

He became silent and said: "You're right, that's how I've been feeling lately. I've been trying to sell my new book and even as the co-founder of the "Chicken Soup for the Soul" brand, I just can't get it sold to a publisher." I answered: "You are not sitting as a king; you are sitting as a servant. And you will be treated as a servant. "

He was ready to change things around in his business. We placed his desk in a power position and within a few months, he had a new big publishing deal and 'The Secret" came into his life. Canfield became one of the top global Motivational Teachers from "The Secret" after my consultation.

You are not following the Principle of Power in the Universe when:

- In your living room, you are sitting with your back to the door watching TV or talking to your family

- In your bedroom, when you wake up, you don't see the door immediately. In your office, you are sitting at a desk, but your back is facing the entrance of your office
- In a restaurant, your back is facing the entrance of the restaurant or your back is facing the door when eating

Solutions:

- Rearrange your couches so you can see the door. Never have someone completely sitting with their back to the incoming flow of energy
- In your bedroom: Place your bed on a wall so you can see your romantic partner coming in. When this is not possible, place a little mirror across the incoming door so you can see who is coming the moment you wake up
- In your office or workspace: Place your desk so you can see people walking in. When this is not possible, place a little mirror to the right or left and in front of you so that it shows you who is coming in from behind you
- Arrive first to your dinner appointment and make sure you can see the door and your guests arriving.

Step 2: Be Supported By the Universe All the Time

When you consider kings, queens and emperors, you realize they are always looking to be supported by a Higher Energy and by their people.

A king or queen will always sit on a throne that supports their back and their neck. Their arms are resting on the chair. You deserve to have the same support.

A true Master of Transformation allows support from the Universe at all times because, without this support, you are unable to fulfil your dreams and manifest your true potential.

Successful people always sit on impressive high-backed chairs. They are not sitting on small chairs without back support.

You are not following the Principle of Power in the Universe when:

- You are sitting on a chair with a low back
- You are sitting on a chair with slats
- You are sitting on an old chair that is falling apart
- You are sitting on the ground or on a pillow
- You are sitting on a couch without support for your back
- You are sleeping in a bed without a headboard or on a mattress on the ground
- You are sleeping in a bed with metal or wooden slats

Solutions:

- Buy a high-backed chair and place it behind your desk, especially when your back is facing the door
- Cover the back of your chair with fabric, or place a pillow between you and the back of the chair
- Remove the old chair and purchase a new one
- Place a headboard at the end of your bed to support your head, or start by placing pillows between your head and the wall
- Place your mattress on top of another mattress, on bricks or anything that brings it 30 cm or a foot from the ground
- Cover the metal and wooden slats with fabric or place pillows against the slats
- When you can't do anything like this, make sure you place support behind you symbolically: a religious, spiritual or philosophical image or statue of support: a Saint or Angel in the Christian tradition, an image of the Letters of God, an image of a Rabbi from the Jewish tradition, the Koran from the Muslim tradition, Gurus from the Hindu tradition, Images of Gods or Goddesses, spiritual Teachers from other Eastern traditions, an image of the CEO or the president of your

company, or just an image of a mountain (make sure it's the mountain isn't completely covered by snow)

- Place a rock, a Buddha statue, or an image of an angel or any other image of support connected with your religious, spiritual or philosophical beliefs behind your home, opposite the front door.
- You can also place a large, round-leaved plant behind you for support.

Step 3: Surround Yourself with Power

The images/statues that are hanging around you represent you. The more powerful the images/statues that are in your home or office, the more you will be treated as a powerful person.

Depending on what you wish to accomplish and in what area you wish to be powerful, your images will be different.

- If you wish to be a powerful scientist, then make sure you hang an image of Einstein or Newton in your living or working space
- If you wish to be an author, place books that have been read for hundreds of years, try Shakespeare

Make sure you resonate with the images. If you don't like the person, don't hang it up.

What are Powerful Images?

- Images of successful people in your profession
- Images of award-winning people connected with your goal
- Images of your idols and heroes, dead or alive
- Images of famous people
- Images of mountains
- Images of your masters, CEO or managers
- Images of your certificates

- Images of Buddha, Jesus, Angels, Saints or Gurus
- Statues of (fake) awards like an Oscar with your name on it
- Front covers with your image on them (even if fake)
- Images of your products in a golden frame
- Images of royal or imperial figures
- Images of people you admire
- Images of your logos, ads, marketing material, articles
- Your vision board with your success goals

Where to Place Your Powerful Images?

- Make sure you have powerful images at the entrance of your company building
- Place them in the North area of your office
- You can hang them behind your chair so you feel supported by powerful people
- You can also hang them in front of where you sit to focus on these successful people
- Place them in your personal success direction. Download the free Marie Diamond app and find out your Personal Energy Number. You will immediately see with the Diamond Compass where your personal success direction is in the room you're standing in
- You can always place your Power affirmation in the North area of your living room, as it will impact all the people living in this home. Or you can place it in the North area of a conference room, and it will create power for the whole company

Step 4: Activate Your Personal Success Direction

You can also place more personal information about your success and abundance in your personal success direction. You can find your personal Success direction in the free Marie Diamond app and you can also go to my website and get your will free energy report.

Extra tips:

- Make sure there is no clutter at the entrance or in the North area of your office
- Remove all images in your home that do not convey power or success

Your Energy Journal

The Diamond Energy Principle of Empowerment

"I Empower All Who I Connect With in the World"

2/ The Diamond Energy Principle of Empowerment

Empowerment is the second Diamond Energy Principle and activates your success. It is the yin aspect of power. You will learn how to activate this within you and in the space around you so that you attract 33% more success.

a/ Your Inner Activation of Empowerment

The word empowerment is one of the trendiest words today. It is definitely a word of the Age of Aquarius. The syllable "em" has the same meaning as "in", so it really means placing yourself or someone else in power or accepting your full potential. Empowerment is helping others grow as human beings and as leaders in their own field.

The past 2500 years was called the Age of Pisces. The political leaders were only empowering themselves and the people were not given any empowerment. Ultimately, the leaders didn't want the people to evolve and grow as human beings. In society, the leaders didn't share any of their power or their tools with the common person. They kept the tools of greatness to themselves.

Although some of this knowledge and wisdom is now surfacing, the people were told that it is sacred, that they were not ready or good enough to receive it. So, it was kept secret. The powerful leaders always knew how to work with the Laws of the Universe, but they didn't want to share it because they were afraid to lose power when they did.

Today, some political leaders still believe that by sharing, they lose power, and so they are still Piscean leaders. They keep the power to themselves and still live in the illusion that this is the best way forward for society. There are individual leaders or groups of leaders who live in this illusion of not sharing power with the people.

But in this Age of Aquarius, empowerment is manifesting as a collective vibration and the old systems no longer work effectively. New systems of empowerment are being created through the use of the internet and social media.

In the last 2500 years, the direction of power was directed towards the leaders of society who demanded all the power and glory. Now we are coming to the age where all power is directed towards you.

Fortunately for humanity, during the Age of Pisces there were political figures who knew that people needed to evolve and so they shared with them the power of education. Leaders who helped their people to read and write were empowering leaders.

But the most empowerment came from figures like Buddha, Jesus, as well as other spiritual and religious leaders who came forward and believed that knowledge and wisdom needed to be shared with the people. They couldn't achieve this as political leaders, but as leaders of Thought and Spirit.

These spiritual leaders empowered us to believe that we are equal in the eyes of God, that we all could reach enlightenment or realize our full human potential. They shared wisdom, tools and information about how to connect with our inner spiritual power.

In the late 18th century, the new thoughts of empowerment started taking place on a political level. And philosophers like Voltaire shared that the power of the political levels needed to become equal not only in spirit but also in form. Unfortunately, when something is suppressed for a long time, it emerges violently. So, the first steps in empowering people on a political level can create sometimes conflicts.

Today we are in a new age of empowerment. Sharing and receiving empowerment from others has become a normal way of living. It is still a grassroots movement, but the internet has definitely helped us empower each other.

Social networking has increased incredibly in the last five years by using tools like YouTube, Instagram, TikTok and other platforms where we can help each other in whatever journey we are on.

The Law of Attraction is working perfectly. You attract the people who are like-minded to your website or social media page so you can feel empowered by the information of transformation.

If information is still withheld by some political elite in some countries, you can find a way to receive it through the internet, which we can really think of as empower-net!

In the last 100 years, many of the new thought thinkers have come forward like Napoleon Hill, Nightingale Conan, the teachers featured in "The Secret", and many others who share how to empower yourself and be the best version of yourself.

One of the most important aspects of this is that you are encouraged by these new thinkers to share the information. That is what true empowerment is; once you know, you don't keep it to yourself. You share it with your partner, your children, your family, and your friends.

That is why "The Secret" was shared with millions of people. Rhonda Byrne and the 24 teachers featured in "The Secret" had the intention to share the secret with you. The energy was set, and it became a snowball that rolled swiftly into society's consciousness.

Be open to receiving transformational tools and wisdom in your life. Ask yourself every day how to become empowered and how to share what you know with others. Some people have to start with sharing what they already know with others and then they start receiving even more. Others, however, need to be open, to receive first as they are the givers of the world.

Be Open to Be Empowered:

- Ask people if they have some empowering words or tools for you
- Share the books that you don't need any more with others and ask if they have some special books or home study courses to share with you that have empowered them
- Listen to your children: they still remember their inner wisdom
- Surf the web, set up your Facebook page or create a website or blog to share your insights with the world
- Talk to the elders in your community or family and ask them what empowered them in their lives
- Take self-help seminars or read the latest self-help books
- Pray for empowerment
- When you download the free Marie Diamond app, you will receive Daily Transformational Messages to empower you to stay focused on Success, Health, Relationships and Inner Wisdom

Diamond Energy Exercise

Take time to relax and close your eyes. Connect within by breathing consciously, in and out. Then visualize that you are in a beautiful space in nature where you feel in complete harmony and peace. Imagine there is a quantum rainbow in the sky with 24 colors. You connect in with the cobalt blue aspect of this rainbow and fill your body and energy field with this color. From your head to your feet, you are filled with the cobalt blue energy of the Universe.

Focus now on your heart chakra in the center of your chest. As you breathe in, think about someone that you wish to empower in your family, your friends or in the world. Radiate the cobalt blue color out from your heart chakra while you breathe out. Imagine that a ray of cobalt blue is reaching the heart of the person you are sending it to. You are radiating this color without expectations or judgments.

Say the following affirmation: ***"I Empower You"*** Focus again on the beautiful space around you in your visualization and open your eyes.

b/ The Diamond Energy Color of Empowerment

The color of empowerment is cobalt blue.

Cobalt blue is the blue color of the night. The night is mysterious. When empowering games are played in fraternities and youth movements, they are done at night when the cobalt blue color is surrounding them.

Have you ever tried to sneak out of the house at night to go for a walk? You really had to tap into your inner power and be courageous in order to conquer your fears. You empowered yourself to go beyond your limits.

Place a cobalt blue item in the North area of your bedroom, living room or office to attract more Empowerment in your life.

How Can You Use This Color, Cobalt Blue?

- Place your awards or trophies or items on a cobalt blue fabric in the North area of your living room or bedroom
- If you have children who are being bullied, you can place their picture in a cobalt blue frame to create more inner power and strength

c/ Your Feng Shui Activation of Empowerment

Being an empowered human means that you are open to transform your life. When you start to change things, make the changes with the right attitude. Move forward without fear and, even if you have the fear, move forward anyway.

When you need to make changes in your life, make them without complaints but with the vision that it will help you to succeed. Accept everything that empowers you, and accept them with happiness and joy.

If people are unjustly criticizing you because they wish to keep you small or close to them, don't be so hard on them. Be compassionate when letting go of things and people. Don't judge them for trying to hold you back, they're just fearful of what will happen to you or that they will lose you. Tell them you will not remain the same person, but you will remain a friend and a loving family member.

When something or someone is no longer helping you attain your vision, it is sometimes time to move on. But you can leave them with grace and gratitude. Never criticize them, just honor them on your path even if you had difficulties with them. Remember that everyone you meet is there at the right time and right place for the perfect reason: your transformational evolution.

When you look at your home and it's not how you really wish it to be, maybe because it is too small, too cluttered, or too unorganized, don't criticize yourself. A home can help you bring your potential forward. So, be grateful for what you have at this time.

Perhaps it is not the million-dollar home you always dreamed about, but it is what you have attracted now. By being grateful for it, you are starting well. Be open to transforming your home by using the suggestions I give you in this chapter.

Has your desk been moved around so you can see the door? Have you changed some of your images already? What are you waiting for? What are you afraid of?

Transforming your life just doesn't happen by sitting and waiting. It requires some action steps.

Even by taking the pictures down and putting them in storage until you find new pictures is a step in the right direction. When I do consultations with people at home, I always take down pictures that don't work well.

It will immediately start working for you, as opposed to keeping the pictures hanging for another week and putting it off.

Try to do some of your suggestions immediately, like within a day or a week. Find a friend who will do the changes with you; an empowering friend. Working with someone else is more fun and you can help each other get over the hurdles of resistance.

When you notice you don't have the things you need to change your environment, ask family or friends if they have something you can use.

I was at a client's house that needed a mirror, and I could feel her resistance. While we were looking at the entrance of her apartment, a neighbor came down the steps with a mirror intended for the garbage. I asked her if she was throwing it away, she said yes, and we immediately had a mirror. The resistance melted away. The Universe was already providing.

When you are looking for new images, find something you like on the Internet, print it out, and frame it until you find an image that is right for your space. It is better to place something small and right than something big and wrong.

Surround Yourself with Empowerment.

- Place a cobalt blue item in the North area of your living room or office to empower your family or team
- You can place images of moments in your life that were empowering to you, like awards or trophies
- You can place ornaments and move furniture with the right attitude. You know that making changes with grace and gratitude in your environment will create more power in your life
- You can have a tribute table where you place awards and trophies
- You can display letters of recognition or pictures of yourself with or among famous and powerful people
- Display front covers of major magazines with your name or face on them. Of course, this may not exist yet, but you can just create them on the Internet and hang them out

Extra tips:

- Always give yourself compliments when you look in the mirror
- When others compliment you, accept it with grace

Your Energy Journal

The Diamond Energy Principle of Abundance

"I Am Abundance in All I Am and in All I Do"

3/ The Diamond Energy Principle of Abundance

Abundance is the third Diamond Energy Principle and activates your Success. You will learn how to activate this within you and in the space around you in order to attract 33% more Success.

a/ Your Inner Activation of Abundance

You are an abundant human being. The word "Abundant" comes from the Latin word "Abundare" which means to abound, like a river that is overflowing with bounty.

Abundance is like an overflowing grail or cup. The universe always provides and there is more than enough for you and everyone else. There are many books written about money and how the Law of Attraction works with money. I will not repeat their information, but I just will add some thoughts to this aspect.

Abundance is about so much more than physical money. Your source of energy is God/the Universe, is present within you and around you and is always abundant. The answers and the insights are always there for you, but you need to open up to the awareness that everything is always there. Even if you can't see it or even if you can't touch it.

Abundance comes from the place where miracles happen. Miracles don't happen by themselves; you need to prepare for them with prayers, focus and actions.

In order to be in that state of abundance, you need first to accept that you are the creator of this abundance. It is your grail that overflows.

You don't need to depend on other people's energy or insights to be abundant, and you don't need to be scared to tap into the abundant being that you are.

Most abundance is created when people are in a deep crisis and ask God for an answer. Then they receive insights or a brilliant idea that makes them abundant. Most people that are in that position will, when financial abundance comes to them, share this abundance with others. The more they share it the more their abundance will increase in spirit and matter.

Consider Oprah Winfrey. When do you think she feels the most abundant? When she had her first million in her bank account or when she was able to share the first million with her charities? Share your abundance.

Even if you don't have a lot of financial abundance, share it. That is what tithing is about. Years ago, I started sharing the largest bank note I had in my wallet with the first beggar I saw on the street every day. He or She is God to me, and I wanted to give back to God. I don't judge whether they're begging for money, for drugs, or for food. It is given because this beggar is God and therefore it is for good.

I was living in the US and was financially struggling. I only had one $100 note in my wallet. That was the only money I had with me at that moment and there was nothing in my bank account. I saw a beggar, the first I saw that day, and I took out my wallet and saw that I didn't have anything smaller than the one $100 note. I opened my wallet, and I gave him that bill.

I blessed it and I knew I was abundant so I would be okay. My husband was very upset until we went to the mailbox that day and I found an unexpected check of $1,000 that I could cash immediately and could provide a full meal for my family. Abundance is always present.

Abundance is for most people seen as financial abundance. Of course, you can do more with a lot of money. It is definitely part of the abundance factor. You can do more good things, with more money. Money is a magnifier. When good is already in your heart, money will magnify your goodness and you will start sharing your abundance. When egoism is already in your heart, you will start acting more egoistic when you have a lot of money.

Abundance is about feeling the unlimited source that is the Universe and accepting that you have constant access to this. It doesn't mean you will have to ask all the time, but you can.

True abundance is having wealth of spirit and matter. Wealth meaning, "We can have it all." You can have abundance of the spirit and abundance of matter.

Abundance of Spirit:

- You have good communication with the Universe/God
- You pray or meditate daily
- You receive the insights and the information when you need it for moving forward on your journey
- You have mentors on your path that help you remember you are the creator of your own abundance

Abundance of Matter:

- You have your own space where you can create your life
- You have sufficient financial funds to live your life as you please
- You have a healthy body
- You have friends and family who help you in times of need

Resistance to Abundance

There are collective cultural blockages that you may have once believed in, such as abundance is only for the few who have power and knowledge, or abundance is only when you are born into a wealthy family.

There are family blockages that you may have taken on from your own parents and family members. I know one of mine was the expression my mother shared with me: "You can't have it all: a good-looking husband and a lot of money."

I repeated this until, I realized that I had found a good-looking husband, but wanted to attain financial freedom too. Do not repeat the expressions of your parents if they create a lack of abundance.
There are also individual notions you created by your own experience in your life. It is possible that you experienced a financial crisis in your business, and you think it will happen again in the future.

It is important to look at all the layers of resistance towards abundance, and then release them in your inner self. They have not suited you to this point, so let go of them.

The first step is to stop thinking the thoughts that have not served you in the past, and each time you have doubts or fears about abundance, connect with the source in yourself knowing that the Universe/God is overflowing in you with the abundance of its/His being.

Be Open to Abundance

- Pay your bills with the gratitude that you have the money to pay them. You can bless them, and more blessings will come to you

- Bless what you have at this moment, even if it doesn't seem like a lot in your eyes, you created it and therefore it is valuable and beautiful. Bless it so you can receive more. The more you bless, the more you open up to abundance
- Look at yourself in the mirror every day and be grateful for the body that holds your spirit in such a perfect way
- Pray and meditate that your grail is overflowing with spirit and matter that serves you on your journey towards abundance
- Listen to people who are abundant and do not envy or criticize them for what they have accomplished

Diamond Energy Exercise

Take time to relax and close your eyes. Connect within by breathing consciously in and out. Then visualize yourself in a beautiful space in nature where you feel in complete harmony and peace. Imagine there is a quantum rainbow in the sky with 24 colors. You connect in with the gold aspect of this rainbow and fill your body and energy field with this color.

From your head to your feet, you are filled with the gold energy of the Universe. As you breathe in, you fill yourself with abundance and as you breathe out you are letting go of every thought, feeling and past action that limited your abundance.

After this you can connect with a situation, a goal or a relationship where you wish to have more abundance and visualize the color gold around and in it, until you feel completely abundant.

Say the following Affirmation: ***"I Am Abundance in All I Am and in All I Do."*** Focus again on the beautiful space around you in your visualization and open your eyes.

b/ The Diamond Energy Color of Abundance

The color of abundance is gold. In all the cultures where a golden era was established, people lived in peace and there was a great culture and trade system. Think about the Egyptian, Greek, and the Roman cultures.

When there is a lot of abundance, humans are showing this by using gold leaves in their paintings and statues, and by using gold in their jewelry.

In archaeology, the use of gold on walls and construction (like a golden dome or golden top) was one of the indications that an ancient culture was abundant. Still today gold is a symbol of wealth. Think about the Oscars, Golden Globes and the Emmy awards: they are all covered with a golden layer. Again, if you are the best, you deserve the gold standard and you will receive a golden award.

Do you have the Midas touch? King Midas was a king who turned everything into gold when he touched it. Well, you are as mighty as Midas and your touch is as powerful. So, bring some gold into your life.

Gold has always been the color associated with the Kings, Queens and Emperors. Achieving the gold standard and having gold medals. Going to the Olympic Games and winning the golden medal is one of the dreams of any athlete.

How Can You Use this Color, Gold?

- You can place Golden items in the entrance of your home to set the gold standard when you enter
- Find out what your Chinese animal sign is and find a golden statue of it, and then place it in your personal best direction

- Wear a golden watch or gold-looking jewelry to attract abundance
- You can also place a wealth ship in the Southeast section of your living area or office. A wealth ship is a model of a ship that you must fill with real gold looking coins (they can be from all over the world), old Chinese coins, old jewelry, fake golden ingots, fake golden bars, or small gemstones
- Make sure you direct the wealth ship sailing into your home and not sailing out of the door. You can also place this wealth ship in your personal success direction in your office

c/ Your Feng Shui Activation of Abundance

The Feng Shui masters focused on creating abundance. I have personally experienced how Feng Shui influences abundance. I have seen this with so many of my clients who increased their income within a year of using my Feng Shui advice.

It doesn't mean that money flows into your home, but that the opportunities to make money do. The following are some general suggestions about how to create more abundance:

- Place a golden looking symbol of money or prosperity in the Southeast of your office, like a gold bowl filled with gold coins
- You can place in the Southeast area of your office, a bubbling fountain
- Place the Chinese God of Wealth or any other image of a deity representing wealth
- Add gold colored or gold looking objects to your environment like vases or candles
- Place your certificates or awards in gold-colored frames
- Place some fake million-dollar bills on your vision board, not just a one-dollar bill. The Universe will give you what you ask for, so make it count

- Place your financial records and important papers in a beautiful cabinet
- Place money frogs with coins in their mouths on the ground in the corners of your office to capture wealth
- Place lush, round-leafed plants in your living room and office
- Place images of yourself and wealthy people in your personal relationship direction

Extra tips:

- Remove all winter landscapes in your home since they show the poverty of energy. Summer and spring landscapes show the abundance of nature, which is what you want to attract
- Place your piggy bank in a closet
- Place magazines talking about wealth and fortune on your coffee table or next to your bed

Your Energy Journal

The Diamond Energy Principle of Magnificence

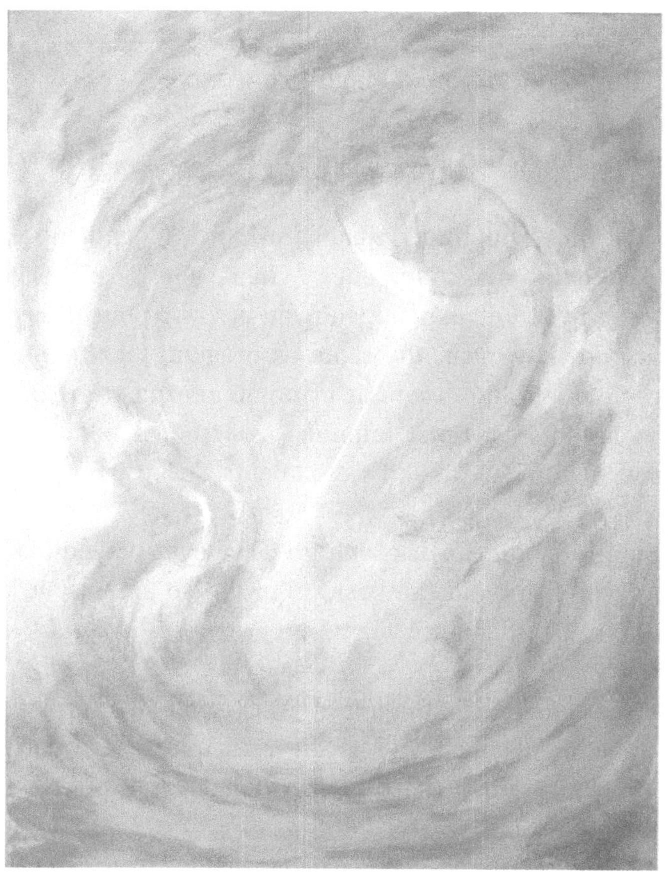

"I See the Magnificence in All That is in the World"

4/ The Diamond Energy Principle of Magnificence

Magnificence is the fourth Diamond Energy Principle and activates your Success. It is the Yin aspect of abundance. You will learn how to activate this within you and in the space around you to attract 33% more success.

a/ Your Inner Activation of Magnificence

To manifest abundance is to magnify what you already have.

The word comes from the original Latin word "Magnificus". It means splendid, noble and eminent. When you are focused on magnificence, you will expand who you are, your business and your life. This does not mean the same as bragging but telling greater truths to yourself and others. It means honoring who you are and sharing your talents. Don't minimize yourself; maximize who you are, and what you have as skills and talents.

For example, if someone asks you if you've ever played piano, don't answer, "Well I just did the basics; I'm not so great at it." Answer instead, "Yes, I studied for 2 years."

Tell the truth and even if the information is not so impressive, share it with maximum effect. This is the principle where you need to honor who you are and what you have done in your life.

Write down all the things you learned in school, from others, or from your own experiences. Write down all the impressive or important people that you've met. You have attracted them all into your life.

Write down all the life lessons you have experienced and all the skills you have acquired. You should be impressed with yourself and rightly so!

I suggest starting a diary where you can note down at least five things every evening that show you've improved yourself in some way.

For example, you became better with your patience; you were able to leave your desk without leaving a mess; you were able to let go of an old painful story, etc.

Every day there are things that you can become more magnificent in. This is one of the things we are here to do: to grow and to learn. Even if we resist this growth process and have growing pains, we still grow and become more magnificent. Give yourself a high five for accomplishing growing and learning.

Once you understand this process, you will be able to receive the compliment from others who are sharing your magnificence. Just accept them as magnificent people do, with grace and gratitude. Start magnifying other people's gifts and talents. The more you encourage people and share with them what is beautiful, glorious, great, and luminous about them, the more they will magnify who you are.

When you are leading a team, it is necessary to magnify their talents, in a reasonably true way. Again, you are not bragging about something that is not there. You are just telling the truth and you maximize this.

Take extra actions, too; for instance, give a certificate, an award, a bouquet of flowers, a picture, or a card. This way, the memory of that moment stays in their lives and when they look at this physical item, they will remember how magnificent they were in your eyes.

Magnificence is the difference between great and greatest. Do you wish to be good at what you do, or do you wish to be the best at what you do?

Do you wish to be a good adviser, or do you wish everyone would see you as the expert, the ultimate standard of advice?

When I was younger, I sang a song with others in the Catholic Church called the "Magnificat." We were sharing the magnificence of God by magnifying Him, which also means magnifying ourselves. You are God within, which is to reflect God's energy in your soul. It is up to you to live from that place of magnificence and to no longer react from your ego that holds you in limitations and scarcity.

You Can Be Open to Magnificence:

- Pray daily for the magnificence that you already have even if it is just a roof over your head and the basic needs. There are still people who have less than you
- Honor the greatness of your body by taking fewer abusive substances like alcohol and drugs
- Take time to enjoy nature
- Stop blaming and criticizing yourself for past events. If you didn't do something right, you can't change it by blaming yourself, but you can change it by learning the lesson and by doing it better next time
- Accept compliments with a smile of gratitude
- Start giving yourself a compliment at least once a day

Diamond Energy Exercise

Take time to relax and close your eyes. Connect within by breathing consciously in and out. Then visualize that you are in a beautiful space in nature where you feel complete in harmony and in peace. Imagine there is a quantum rainbow in the sky with 24 colors. You connect in with the silver aspect of this rainbow and fill your body and energy field with this color. From your head to your feet, you are filled with the Silver energy of the Universe.

Focus now on your heart chakra in the center of your chest. As you breathe in, think about someone that you wish to magnify the abundance for in your family, your friends or in the world. Radiate the silver color out from your heart chakra while you breathe out. Imagine that a ray of silver is reaching the heart of the person you are sending it to. You are radiating this color without expectations or judgments.

Say the following affirmation: ***"I See the Magnificence in You"***. Focus again on the beautiful space around you in your visualization and open your eyes.

b/ The Diamond Energy Color of Magnificence

The color of magnificence is silver. Silver is one of the colors that is connected with wealth. The kings and queens loved having silver details on their clothing or on their shoes. They are surrounding them with silver chandeliers, and silverware polished to perfection. The more their outfits and surroundings are shining, the more they expand their wealth. It activates what you already have. When you live in poverty you don't want to double how things look around you.

Get a silver mirror for your personal bag or a large silver framed mirror in your home. Doubling your dining room shows that you are not afraid to double the magnificence of who you are and the life you live.

Have you ever seen the sunlight radiate on a lake with the silver energy of the water that simply took your breath away? A silver lake is an astounding view. You can also encounter this kind of magnificence when the full moon is on the ocean and you walk along the shore. This is magnificence.

How Can You Use This Color Silver?

- Wear a silver belt or carry a silver purse on a night out
- Place some fake silver flowers in a vase in the Northwest of your living room, especially in the winter
- Place a silver item in the Northwest of your office

c/ Your Feng Shui Activation of Magnificence

Ask everyone in your home or office to clean up on a weekly basis, and later on a daily basis. Before you start your day, make your bed so you can go to sleep in a bed that is not messy and that is inviting when you go to sleep.

Make sure to clean your desk before you go home so that you will start better the next day. Other steps to increase your magnificence are the following:

- You can put silver items in the Northwest area of your living room
- Polish your crystal chandeliers
- Polish your silverware
- Place candles in silver candle holders
- Keep shoes, coats, and accessories hidden in a closet or wardrobe
- Hang a crystal chandelier in your entrance or in your dining room
- Hang a mirror with a silver frame to reflect your dining table
- Make sure there are no clothes or other items lying on the ground and creating a mess

Extra Tips:

- Bring out your good china every Sunday for lunch or for a special family occasions
- Dress up every day, the more you look magnificent and excellent, the more the Universe will bring what you focus on

Your Energy Journal

The Diamond Energy Principle of Joy

"I Am Joy in All I Am and in All I Do"

5/ The Diamond Energy Principle of Joy

Joy is the fifth Diamond Energy Principle and activates your Success. You will learn how to activate this within you and in the space around you to attract 33% more Success.

a/ Your Inner Activation of Joy

The game that is called life can only be really enjoyable if there is Joy in it. I can't help sometimes thinking God/the Universe has to have some Joy in this process of evolution and seeing His creation unfold. I am sure God sometimes smiles like the Mona Lisa, mysteriously but with intention, or that God sometimes bursts out in laughter as if watching the funny jokes of late-night talk shows.

Joy is a very important part of mastering the law of attraction. If you don't have Joy, what do you have? I see too many people being too serious in this game called life. How long has it been since you've burst out in laughter about yourself and what life has brought you or at least smiled about the goofy moments in your life.

When I see people in seminars all over the world, I feel as though I need to brighten up their lives. They are too serious. I try to be a spiritual stand-up comedian and make my audience laugh. Enjoy this wild ride called life!

All the beauty created in this Universe is to make you full of joy. I do understand that life is sometimes very stressful, but it is in these times you need to go back to nature or play with children in order to tap into the joy of life.

I know the Universe is joyful because just as we are created in its reflection. As children we have an inherent possibility to be joyful within a few minutes of any major stressful situation.

As a mother raising three children (two boys and one daughter), I am, like any mom, a good practitioner in making children laugh fast because you don't want them to stay crying. Tickling almost always works, showing them a beautiful butterfly outside, making funny faces, or telling them a funny story.

Real joy fills up the space between the experiences of life. It juices up your life and makes your light sparkle again. You don't need a lot of it to be good for the rest of the day, but it needs to be there.

When you start to become aware of the process of Transformation, it takes some time to really see the results. But one of the stepping stones is to start feeling joyful and grateful about what is going to happen even if you don't see it happen yet.

Joy is the wave the Universe surfs on. That is why we love comedians, comedies and clowns. We all need a certain amount of joy to keep us surfing the wave of life. If you wish to excel in Transformation, you need to be able to have access to a source of joy in yourself and be supported by a joyful home or workspace.

Joy is something you need to practice. Most people have forgotten true joy. Transformation works much better if you focus on your goals with joy in your heart. If you put seriousness or strictness in your heart the Universe will give back exactly what you are looking for. You will receive your goals, but without joy.

You Can Be Open to Joy:

- Watch the sunrise every morning and the sunset every evening, enjoy the colors and the multiple aspects of it every day. One of my rituals is to be up at dawn just to see the unfolding beauty of nature.
- Surround yourself with truly joyful people. If you have relationships with people that do not laugh, then perhaps

you need to reconsider if they are the right people to live with

- Follow a little butterfly in its flight through your garden
- Walk in nature to see how the animals react to your presence
- Play daily with your pets
- Put on music and dance
- Sing in the shower no matter what anyone says about your voice
- Eat your favorite food in your favorite restaurant with your best friends

Diamond Energy Exercise

Take time to relax and close your eyes. Connect within by breathing consciously in and out. Then visualize yourself in a beautiful space in nature where you feel in complete harmony and peace. Imagine there is a quantum rainbow in the sky with 24 colors. You connect in with the peach aspect of this rainbow and fill your body and energy field with this color.

From your head to your feet, you are filled with the peach energy of the Universe. As you breathe in, you fill yourself with joy and as you breathe out you are letting go of every thought, feeling and past action that limited your Inner Joy.

After this you can connect with a situation, a goal or a relationship where you wish to have more inner joy and visualize the color peach around and in it, until you feel completely joyful.

Say the following affirmation: ***"I Am Joy in All I Am and in All I Do."*** Focus again on the beautiful space around you in your visualization and open your eyes.

b/ The Diamond Energy Color of Joy

The color of joy is peach. Have you ever eaten a ripe peach and the juice just pours over your face? Either you can be frustrated or start laughing. That is how working with the Universe is like: either you are frustrated that it is not happening fast enough, or you focus on gratitude and imagine how you will feel when it will manifest.

I have recently met a wonderful woman and her second name was Joy. Everywhere there were peach colors in her home; her whole outfit was mostly peach.

I told her that this color stands for her name. The energy in her home was very light and joyful. Enjoy your life by adding more peach colors.

How Can You Use This Color, Peach?

- Peach is an underused color in interior design. It is a great color to lift up your sofa with peach-colored pillows. It always brings extra sparkle, and you will receive many compliments
- Place an image of a bouquet of peach-colored flowers at your entrance or real peach colored rose flowers on your dining table

c/ Your Feng Shui Activation of Joy

It is good Feng Shui to have order in your home, but you need to experience some joy in your home. A home is a living energy. So, don't make your home too serious, or too much of a temple or a monastery.

If you don't laugh enough in your life then, there is something wrong. You have to at least smile several times a day and occasionally burst out into laughter.

Surround Yourself with Joy:

- Place something peach in the West area of your bedroom to keep a joyful relationship with your romantic partner
- Have summer colors in your interior like yellow, peach, orange, and rose
- Hang an image of peach blossoming tree in the West section of your living area
- Have colorful artwork and fabrics in your home
- Hang funny items or pictures in your family room
- Have images of your children playing in the West area of your living room or family room
- Have toys out in your family room
- Avoid images of sadness or crying clowns
- Have moving objects out on your patio like mobiles and wind chimes
- Avoid too many dark colors in your environment like blacks and dark browns
- Hang crystals at your large windows that create rainbows on your walls

Extra tips:

- In China, they place a laughing Buddha, the one with the big belly, at the entrance to make the worries go away and open the hearts for joy. Don't forget to rub the belly often
- Don't forget that joy is not only in images but also in music. Play music that makes you feel joyful and want to dance. Sing along to your favorite music at least once a day

Your Energy Journal

The Diamond Energy Principle of Celebration

"I Celebrate All That is in the World"

6/ The Diamond Energy Principle of Celebration

Celebration is the sixth Diamond Energy Principle and activates your Success. It is the yin aspect of joy. You will learn how to activate this within you and in the space around you to attract 33% more Success.

a/ Your Inner Activation of Celebration

Look back at your life and at all the celebrations you attended. It started for most of us when we were born. Your parents and family celebrated your arrival by visiting you at the hospital or at home and by giving you gifts like toys and clothes. Perhaps you were then celebrated to become a member of a spiritual or religious community by being baptized. In every religion, celebrations are created to honor God.

If you ask most people what their favorite time of the year is they will most likely say Christmas. But it is the celebration of the birth of a great spiritual leader named Jesus and in the Pagan traditions it is the celebration of the winter solstices, when the darkness fades away and when Light returns to nature.

In Pagan traditions, they celebrate spring and summer before the season happens. Celebrate your goals before you have achieved them. When you make a personal vision board, celebrate the goals you posted even if they haven't manifested yet. After you have hung your vision board, celebrate with your family the manifestation that will happen with a dinner, a glass of Champagne or a nice tea with cookies.

Celebrate the coming victories as if they have already happened. Celebrate your first million, not by spending it, but by celebrating it in your mind and heart.

Celebration is using the Law of Gratitude. Celebrate that you have the opportunity to make your first million this year, celebrate that you are able to attract a wonderful romantic partner. Celebrate your health that you will have in a few months or celebrate your new weight before you start dieting.

Celebration can be done in a physical way, but you need to celebrate by feeling the greatness and the gratitude in your heart. Sing Hallelujah before the miracle has happened.

But remember that besides celebrating your own possible manifestations, you need to share with others that you celebrate them being in your life. Women are happy when a man comes home with a bouquet of flowers not because they want something or because they have done something wrong but because they want to celebrate on an ordinary day, that they love their wife.

Celebration is something that people do when efforts are accomplished and when you know the result. But true masters of the Universal laws know that you need to celebrate every moment of your life. As you celebrate life itself, life will celebrate you. That is why it is so important to visualize the awards before you receive them in your reality.

You have so much to be grateful for, but don't let gratitude only be in your heart. Express it in all the ways you can. Don't wait for it. Immediately plan a party after reading this chapter. Just reading this book is a good excuse; put music on and start dancing!

Let your heart overflow with joy. Your Soul wants to express this inner joy. Rituals are a form of celebration of the soul, which is why ancient cultures and religions have created rituals to celebrate Life.
A ritual opens a connection through symbolism, through music, and words with the celebratory level of your Soul. When you celebrate from your Soul, candles, incense and flowers can be part of the

celebration. I always feel that we celebrate when we dress up and bring in our loved ones and friends to be part of it.

You Can Be Open to Celebration:

- Light candles when you arrive home
- Place a fresh bouquet of flowers at your entrance
- Surround yourself with friends and family to celebrate your next birthday
- Express grace and gratitude before every meal

Diamond Energy Exercise

Take time to relax and close your eyes. Connect within by breathing consciously in and out. Then visualize yourself in a beautiful space in nature where you feel in complete harmony and peace. Imagine there is a quantum rainbow in the sky with 24 colors. You connect in with the orange aspect of this rainbow and fill your body and energy field with this color. From your head to your feet, you are filled with the orange energy of the Universe.

Focus now on your heart chakra in the center of your chest. As you breathe in, think about someone that you wish to celebrate in your family, your friends or the world. Radiate the orange color out from your heart chakra while you breathe out. Imagine that a ray of orange is reaching the heart of the person you are sending it to. You are radiating this color without expectations or judgments.

Say the following Affirmation: ***"I Celebrate You"***. Focus again on the beautiful space around you in your visualization and open your eyes.

b/ The Diamond Energy Color of Celebration

The color of celebration is orange. In China, they have many colors of celebration like red and gold. But in every home, you will find bowls of oranges to celebrate joyful abundance. When I was a child, my mother told me that when she was a small girl oranges were very rare and it was on a festivity for the celebration of St. Nicolas on December 6th when they each received one orange.

Now oranges are easy to buy, but I still think that freshly squeezed orange juice in the morning is a celebratory moment.

How Can You Use This Color Orange?

- Place orange pillows on your couch to celebrate your family life
- You can place a bowl with fresh oranges or mandarins on your breakfast table to celebrate every new morning or have a fresh orange juice for breakfast
- When you go out to celebrate, wear something orange, even if it is socks or an accessory. People will feel your celebratory mood

c/ Your Feng Shui Activation of Celebration

I am sure that you have received awards in the past. Even letters from satisfied clients are symbols of celebration. What have you done with them?

I have seen too many golden records, posters of successful movies, images of joy and celebration hanging in the bathroom, on the fridge or hiding in the closet. Do you think that will support you? Make sure you give your awards a special place like a wall of fame or a hall of fame, because you are worth it. This celebrates your potential, your talents and who you are.

Surround Yourself With Celebration:

- Place an orange item in the South area of your living room or office
- Have musical instruments displayed in the East area of your family room
- Hang images of birds placed in the South area of your home
- Place your awards in a visible place, in a special cabinet in your office or in your living room. If you know what your personal success area is, you can place them there
- Place a bowl of fruit in your dining room, especially oranges
- Bring orange candles out when you have a party or even just for yourself
- Give orange flowers to celebrate someone's success
- You can place an image of a tree with oranges, peaches or mandarins in your garden

Extra Tips:

- Make sure you celebrate daily by giving yourself compliments and high fives when you have accomplished something great
- Create an award book where you give yourself a daily award
- Have an award map for your children with symbols of little suns and cakes when they have done their best

Your Energy Journal

B. Transform your Health

To help enhance your health and wellbeing, there are six Diamond Energy Principles that you can activate. These principles are:

- Healing
- Honesty
- Purity
- Transparency
- Forgiveness
- Release

You will encounter details about these principles in the next chapter

The Diamond Energy Principle of Healing

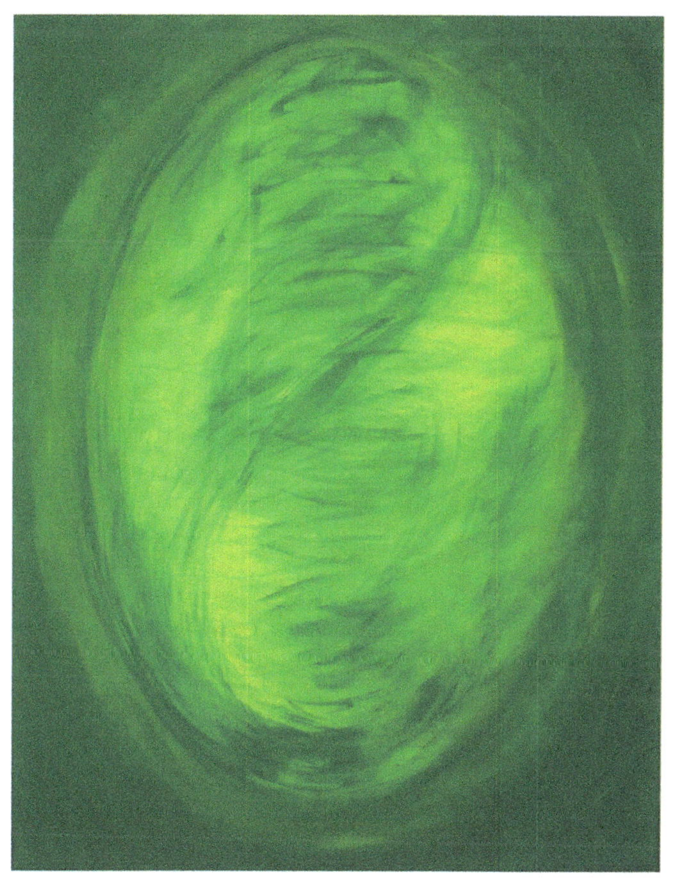

"I Am Healing in All I Am and in All I Do"

1/ The Diamond Energy Principle of Healing

Healing is the seventh Diamond Energy Principle and activates your Health and Wellbeing. You will learn how to activate this within you and in the space around you to attract 33% more Health.

a/ Your Inner Activation of Healing

The word "Healing" has again the word all in it. As you are the Universe within you, you have the wholeness of all solutions in yourself. Anything that you have created in yourself, which takes you away from the awareness that you are all, you can restore by connecting in with that quantum field that is the Universe. You have created lacks and blockages through your thoughts, feelings, actions and sometimes in previous lifetimes as well.

The reason why you are not experiencing wholeness anymore can be complex, and a Master of the Law of Attraction doesn't focus on the past anymore but lives in the wholeness of their being in the present. Everyone has this healing power and many healing modalities referring to this healing power in you. I became aware of my healing power after a major accident at fifteen years old when my skin was totally destroyed. I really looked like a monster. I remember my mother didn't want to give me a mirror and she said that perhaps I would need plastic surgery one day.

I told her to never sign a paper for this, that I would heal myself. So, I started to put my hands on my face many hours a day and within 14 days my face looked radiant and I had beautiful skin, that many complimented me and still to this day. I learned later on that I did Reiki on myself. Reiki is a healing modality where you connect in with the Chi of the Universe and allow it to flow through your hands.

I believe in uniting all the healing modalities with each other. I believe that the Eastern healing practices are fabulous, but the

Universe has also given us the modern Western practices because they are an answer to problems we are facing at this moment. You can prevent and support yourself with many Eastern and homeopathic healing practices, but it is also great to have a modern doctor to see if your bone is broken and help restore it. Find the right balance between all the modalities to support your health.

In ancient cultures, healers had the gift of seeing energy. They didn't need x-rays because their eyes could see into the energy field around someone. There are still healers in the world who have remained with this healing power, but there are not enough around to help all of humanity.

When you have an attitude that you will heal, you will more likely attract a better doctor and a better healing modality than if you have the attitude that you can't heal when you have a major disease.

Know that you can attract healing. You can ask for anything from the Universe. Keep focusing that you will heal, and it is more likely that this will happen.

Healing doesn't always focus on the physical level. Healing can happen on the emotional, mental, and even spiritual level. One level always affects the other levels of your being.

The best results will occur if you bring together all the levels in a healing mode: physical, emotional, mental, and spiritual. We have all the possibilities available. It would be a great change if all the different healers could work together: the modern doctor with the Qigong master, the surgeon with the Reiki master and the dowser with the cardiologist. What a perfect world would that be?

Diamond Energy Exercise

Take time to relax and close your eyes. Connect within by breathing consciously in and out. Then visualize yourself in a beautiful space in nature where you feel in complete harmony and peace. Imagine there is a quantum rainbow in the sky with 24 colors. You connect in with the emerald green aspect of this rainbow and fill your body and energy field with this color.

From your head to your feet, you are filled with the emerald green energy of the Universe. As you breathe in, you fill yourself with healing and as you breathe out you are letting go of every thought, feeling and past action that limited your inner healing.

After this you can connect with a situation, a goal or a relationship where you wish to have more healing and visualize the color emerald green around and in it, until you feel it is completely healed. Say the following Affirmation: ***"I Am Healing in All I Am and in All I Do."*** Focus again on the beautiful space around you in your visualization and open your eyes.

2/ The Diamond Energy Color of Healing

The color of healing is emerald green. When I was fifteen years old, I had a major accident. I survived but with a lot of health issues. I had only 20 percent of my short-term memory. For about ten years I was in bed more than out. So, health was a real issue until I was twenty-five years old. I had the good fortune to live in a home surrounded by trees and a beautiful garden.

So, whenever I felt low in energy I walked in the garden, connecting in with the trees and the flowers. But, in retrospect, I did something else that at that time I didn't understand very well. I desired to wear green outfits. When I had to study for tests, I put on my favorite green outfit that I had for ten years: a short skirt and polo in emerald green. I otherwise never wore such a color.

When you read on, you will understand that emerald green is a healing color and it creates good health for us. It is the color of nature where all the healing power is.

In traditional Chinese culture, good health is seen as more important than great romance. That is why the Chinese take such good care of themselves by doing Tai Chi, Qigong or by taking Chinese herbs. Longevity is one of the life goals for the Chinese people.

You only start understanding how important it is when you start losing it. A home can definitely inspire good health. The ancient Feng Shui Masters bring two aspects together to create good health: having good Feng Shui and sleeping or living where there is no Geopathic stress. The ancient paintings showed Feng Shui masters with a compass and with dowsing rods.

Emerald green is the color that inspires health. It relates with nature and with the source of health, we experience it by connecting in with the treasures that are in nature: air, plants, trees, quietness and relaxation.

How Can You Use This Color, Emerald Green?

- Place lush green plants in your living room or family room, but make sure you don't place them in your bedroom since they create too much active energy during the nighttime
- Wear emerald green as a part of your outfit, even as an accessory, if you feel you can use this color to support your health

c/ Your Feng Shui Activation of Healing

Health can be represented in many ways in your life.
To have health, you need to make sure you are in balance. When you overdo things in one area of your life, you don't have enough energy for the other areas.

Most women and men today are focusing on success and relationships. Health is not one of their favorite topics until they're confronted with lack of health and wellbeing. Health issues can be mental problems, anxiety, emotional depression, or sudden physical problems or life-threatening diseases.

Feng Shui is about balance between yin and yang (passive and active – night and day). You need to balance the active part and the passive part of your life; you need time to sleep and relax. All the hours that you don't relax will accumulate and before you know it, you will create something in your health that demands you start relaxing and sleeping the hours you've been missing.

In order to have great health you also need to have the right health team in place around you. The best doctor, healer, massage therapist, chiropractor, etc. If you don't need them, great, but if you do, you need the best that are available. Focusing on great health is also to attract the right people to support you with this.

Health is also about prevention by taking supplements, maintaining a healthy diet, walking in nature, doing breathing exercises, meditating, or anything that can keep your health perfect.

Surround Yourself with Healing Energy:

- Place a green item in the East area of your bedroom, office or living room to attract more good health in your life
- Balance passive and active areas in your home. For instance, certain rooms should be quiet while others should be active
- Have the five elements in your home: water, wood, fire, earth, and metal
- Have images of lush green flowers and gardens, but avoid cacti or plants with pointy leaves
- Have the bathroom door always closed so that the flushing energy of the toilet is not connected with the living areas
- Hang wind chimes in your garden.

- Have books on healing laying on your nightstand
- Have images of people walking, running, or doing exercises, but not in your bedroom
- Always place fresh flowers in your living room; never dead flowers or potpourri
- Store away all sharp objects like knives, scissors and weapons
- Place all garbage bins in a closet

Activate the Health of Your Whole Family:
In the East area of your family or living room, place a bamboo plant or a lush green plant.

Activate Balance in Your Home:
Play soft background music and place a large white quartz crystal on the coffee table in your living room.

Activate Your Home for Attracting a Good Doctors and Healers:
In the Northwest of your office or living room, place business cards or information about the team that will help you create excellent health.

Activate Your Personal Health Direction:
You can also place more personal information about your health, your medicine or books about healing in your personal health direction.

Extra Tips:

- Always travel with some healing books to read
- Open the windows an hour before you go to sleep so you can let in fresh air
- Walk daily to create wellbeing

Your Energy Journal

The Diamond Energy Principle of Honesty

"I Am Honest in All My Actions in the World"

2/ The Diamond Energy Principle of Honesty

Honesty is the eight Diamond Energy Principle and activates your health and wellbeing. You will learn how to activate this within you and in the space around you to attract 33% more health.

a/ Your Inner Activation of Honesty.

In order to be healthy, it is important that you check in with yourself and face the truth about your health. Regardless of your age, are you healthy in body, mind, and soul?

Truth is about being honest to yourself and not making any excuses anymore. A Master in Transformation is totally honest with themselves. It's okay if you made some mistakes in your life, but at least admit it to yourself. That is the first step, and then you can start sharing with others that you feel comfortable with your personal truth.

I was reading an article in Oprah's magazine about people who had been sexually abused and kept it to themselves for more than thirty years. They kept the pain in their hearts and souls, and they kept it from their loved ones. It's heart-breaking, but the truth sets you free. When they were able to finally share this honestly with their family, the healing process could start. It didn't mean that they were healed at once, though, because keeping the truth hidden for so long will take a longer process to recuperate. But the sooner you can share old pain and unhealthy situations with people you feel safe with, the better it is for you.

Sometimes you will have pushed the truth so deep down in yourself that you don't even remember it consciously, but your body remembers and so does your heart.

I remember that I always felt pain in my neck when I got too stressed. One day I told myself that I wanted to know the truth about this pain. I asked my unconsciousness to release the truth. When you ask, you will receive the information: in a dream, a vision or a memory that just pops up.

You might even read about a similar story or see someone on Dr. Phil talking about their own story and you will instantly know - that it is just like you.

After one week of asking for the truth, I got in contact with a homeopath and she gave me some homeopathic remedies. Within a few days, I had such a bad reaction that I started crying and being hysterical, but my husband guided me and took care of me. He told me that I was remembering, and while holding me in his arms I allowed the memory to come back.

My father, in rage, had tried to kill me when I was seven years old because I knew something horrible about him. He tried to choke me and said that if I didn't shut up about this, he would definitely kill me the next time. That imprint had connected with my neck. After that revealing memory came back, I never had that kind of pain in my neck again.

Of course, I also forgave my father. I understood now that I was, apparently, a big threat to him. For some reason, I kept this under the radar for so long so that I could learn from the experience and share it now with you.

In organizations where they support people to release addictions, honesty is crucial. The first thing people need to share in the group session is to say hello, say their name, and admit what they're addicted to. Only then can the healing begin. It is important for you therefore to understand that when you wish to heal your life on all levels, whether physical, emotional, mental, financial, or spiritual, you need to be honest with yourself and say, "Okay, I made a mess of this. It is time to heal now."

Do this from an observant place and not from a judgmental place. Put on paper the things you have created and know then what needs to be changed.

The Universe/God is not a being of revenge, but rather it is an energy field of compassion. So, come clean with yourself. Again, you don't have to scream it out to the world what your truth is, but as you are the Universe within, you need to be honest with yourself. Your ego will always bend the stories and the excuses toward what feels good for you and will keep the survival going. For instance, "it's okay to have an addiction to alcohol because in my country everyone drinks after work in the pub, and we are all a little bit tipsy before we go home." Or "it is okay to be depressed, look at the world and how depressing it is!"

When you change and be honest with yourself, you will affect everyone around you. Being honest is about being truthful to your highest self. The word, "honest" comes from the Latin word "Honestus", which means "honorable, respected".

The Universe has its codes of honor too. They are called the Laws of the Universe. When you are honoring them, you will receive honest answers. It is quite simple.

The first thing you need to do is start listening to your inner life. Too many people are so busy listening to what is outside of them that they cannot hear their inner voice. If only you could see how many thoughts are spinning in your mind and how many feelings you experience each day. If all of these were printed automatically on paper every second and every minute, you would have thousands of papers coming out of your printer with a chaos of thoughts and feelings.

But guess what? This happens in the ether. All the thoughts and emotions that you, as an ego, produce is in fact, printed out in the Universe and it manifests those thoughts and feelings. Because of this, it is necessary to only think about what you really want, to feel positive, and to expect the best for yourself.

And your soul is giving you advice too; here and there a sentence, an insight, a feeling of peace, a vision, or a dream, but they often get lost in the thousands of thoughts and emotions you have.

Therefore, in order to really be connected with the truth of your soul, you need to become silent, mentally and emotionally, so that you can see or hear or feel the truth of your soul.

Meditating, walking in nature, listening to the sounds of birds, sailing on a lake or ocean, skiing in the high mountains in the silence of the snow, or praying alone in a church; these are moments when the soul has given you information and shared with you the truth about who you really are.

Rarely does anyone get an "aha!" moment in the busy streets of New York or during the rush hours on the tubes of London, between the thousands of people hopping on and off the trains. But going into Central Park in New York or Hyde Park in London is where silence can be experienced.

We all need that truthful time to understand who we are. I encourage you to take time for truth.

You Can Be Open to Truth:

- By smelling the roses every day, whenever you see them
- By arranging a retreat with your pastor or your spiritual teacher
- By starting conversations with your coach, personal therapist, or close friend about the meaning of your life

- By keeping a diary and writing honestly about yourself

Diamond Energy Exercise

Take time to relax and close your eyes. Connect within by breathing consciously in and out. Then visualize yourself in a beautiful space in nature where you feel in complete harmony and peace. Imagine there is a quantum rainbow in the sky with 24 colors. You connect in with the citrus green aspect of this rainbow and fill your body and energy field with this color. From your head to your feet, you are filled with the citrus green energy of the Universe.

Focus now on your heart chakra in the center of your chest. As you breathe in, think about someone that you need honest answers from in your family, your friends or in the world. Radiate the citrus green color out from your heart chakra while you breathe out. Imagine that a ray of citrus green is reaching the heart of the person you are sending it to. You are radiating this color without expectations or judgments.

Say the following affirmation: ***"I Ask for Honesty in you."*** Focus again on the beautiful space around you in your visualization and open your eyes.

2/ The Diamond Energy Color of Honesty

The color of honesty is citrus green. Citrus is, in my Dutch language, close to citron, which stands for lemon. Drinking water with lemon in the morning helps clean and purify your body.

Many years ago, I was invited to a wedding celebration. Some students that were following my meditation course were invited and I felt I should wear citrus green, the color of honesty that night. So, I shopped until I found a gorgeous citrus green outfit.

What I didn't know was that some of my male students wanted to test me to see if I was a true Master. The table was set up in such a way that my husband and I were separated and that I was sitting between two of my male students and my husband between two of my female students.

I immediately felt very uneasy. Within a half hour these two male students were touching me inappropriately, and apparently, the same thing was happening to my husband. I became very angry and insisted that I sit with my husband. I told them how dishonorable they were to play this game with me. I know now that wearing the color citrus green showed me more quickly the dishonesty around me and the dishonorable situation.

How Can You Use This Color Citrus Green?

- Wear a citrus green outfit if you wish to find out the truth about a situation
- Place a citrus green candle and light it with the intention of knowing the truth in the East area of your living room, or in your personal relationship direction

c/ Your Feng Shui Activation of Honesty

We make so many excuses with our ego. We always have a reason to say that something is too hard, that it requires too much discipline and work. Connect with the honor in yourself, stay true to your vision and to the Laws of the Universe and everything will work out. Put up some rules for living with yourself and with others in your home and be completely honest when they don't work or when they need to improve themselves.

Surround Yourself with Honesty:

- You can place citrus green images or items in the East area of your living room or family room
- Have images or statues of dragons in your home
- Have images or statues of elephants in your home
- Keep the center of your home open and spacious
- Don't put heavy furniture in the center of a room
- Include images of honorable people in your home
- Have images or books connected with honorable causes, like those promoted by non-profits and other organizations to heal the world

Extra Tips:

- Remove covers from your sofa or couches instead of hiding things
- Avoid hanging up photos or artwork that reflects negativity

Your Energy Journal

The Diamond Energy Principle of Purity

"I Am the Purity in All I Am and in All I Do"

3/ The Diamond Energy Principle of Purity

Purity is the ninth Diamond Energy Principle activates your health and wellbeing. You will learn how to activate this within you and in the space around you to attract 33% more health.

a/ Your Inner Activation of Purity

Purity comes from the Latin word for pure, "Purus", meaning clear, empty, cloudless, and undecorated. Making something pure means to clean up.

Your Soul is a pure vessel and a reflection of the Universe/God. But the form that expresses the soul is called the material body, and the energetic aura field does not remain pure during the lifetime of incarnation. This state of purity is difficult to maintain though, because negative thoughts and feelings that you create for yourself makes it impure.

My spiritual Master told me that the body becomes impure from actions, judgments, and the limitations that you create. In fact, even the words you use to express frustrations, like curse words, are lower vibrations and can create impure energy fields in your aura field. My Master also shared with me that even though a person may wash with the best soap and use an array of sweet-smelling perfumes, their energy field still smells bad because they use foul language constantly in their sentences.

Many young women will wear makeup; beautiful red lipstick and eye shadow, but the energy in their aura fields around their eyes and lips are dark because of the judgments they make against other people in the form of gossip and criticism.

Purity starts with how you feel inside about yourself. It is important that you try to stay in the innocent state of mind of a small baby.

This is not about being naive but about connecting with the purity of God.

Angels are viewed as beings that represent purity. You can sometimes say that someone is like an angel and if you could see their aura field, you would see that there is a lot of white energy around them. Spiritual and religious leaders sometimes represent themselves with a white dress to show their followers that they have chosen to represent the purity of God. Of course, wearing white is not a guarantee of anyone's inner purity!

The more you live in the purity of yourself and stop judging others and yourself, the faster you will attract great results in success and especially in your health.

Remember that when the Universe is not returning your calls and not fulfilling your orders, don't start doubting or blaming. Just clean up, and uplift yourself and the vibration of the space around you.

Diamond Energy Exercise

Take time to relax and close your eyes. Connect within by breathing consciously in and out. Then visualize yourself in a beautiful space in nature where you feel in complete in harmony and peace. Imagine there is a quantum rainbow in the sky with 24 colors. You connect in with the white aspect of this rainbow and fill your body and energy field with this color.

From your head to your feet, you are filled with the white energy of the Universe. As you breathe in, you fill yourself with purity and as you breathe out you are letting go of every thought, feeling and past action that limited your inner purity.

After this you can connect with a situation, a goal or a relationship where you wish to have more purity in and visualize the color white around and inside until you feel it is completely pure.

Say the following affirmation: ***"I am the Purity in All I Am and in All I Do."*** Focus again on the beautiful space around you in your visualization and open your eyes.

b/ The Diamond Energy Color of Purity

The color of purity is white. Before I studied Feng Shui, I once lived in a home for two years where the level of energy was not pure. This home had seen some sad moments in the past; for instance, a former owner had drowned in the ocean. The entrance of the home was at the North side and many high trees were surrounding it.

Only in the summer did we have enough sunlight coming in. It was a dark home. I felt very depressed there and I could neither focus nor summon up the energy to clean up the clutter.

After a while, I started adding lamps and candles in the corners. I swapped my dark couches for white sofas. I started wearing white and pastel-colored outfits, and I started feeling so much better.

I had managed to regain my focus and my home looked neat and tidy. I found a cleaning product with lavender essential oil in it and started cleaning everything with it.

The aura field of the home became bright. I sprayed lavender mist around me every day. I even started liking the home. I became very clear about what I wanted to do with my life and after we left that home, my career as a Transformational teacher started.

Saints, angels and spiritual teachers are always represented in art by wearing a white dress. It is as if the dress represents the white aura field around them. Aura fields can be seen because what is inside of you will radiate outward and show your true colors.

When you learn about different cultures and religions, white is used often to show a new beginning. At baptisms, marriages and even funerals, white is worn as part of the ceremony. Perhaps it is because white represents the moment that people try to be pure with the intention to let go of the ego.

In Diamond Feng Shui I suggest people wear more white clothes, especially around the heart. Too many people wear dark colored outfits. Lighten up your wardrobe and your closet. I stopped wearing black after my spiritual teacher had asked me to wear head-to-toe black for six months back when I was 20.

During this time, I became very depressed and I attracted very strange boyfriends and strange energy experiences. I begged him to change colors. He smiled and asked me to start wearing more light-colored outfits.

How Can You Use This Color White?

- Place some white flowers on your coffee table like a white orchid
- Place an image of a white angel hanging above or near the front door to tell the Universe that you've chosen to have an uplifting and pure energy field

c/ Your Feng Shui Activation of Purity

If you've already made changes to your home using the information in this book, but you haven't yet received any major changes, it can be a sign that you need to take care of the level of purity that is in your home. Purity can be measured by the level of light that you have in your home or office.

Universal energy is reflected in the white light of the sun, therefore you need to have a certain amount of real light in the rooms of your home. If you cannot have real sunlight coming in, then you need to fake it and make sure there is electric or candlelight in the darker areas.

The Universe requires a vessel to send in your gifts. Light is a vessel of transportation. The quality of light in your home or office will influence the ease for the Universe to bring in your requests.

The word "light," however, is more than visual light. It is also the etheric field of your home. Your home is light, if it feels light. You can feel the opposite of light if you enter somewhere and feel like you can't breathe, feel uneasy, or something else is bothering you.

You may not be able to really tell what it is, but you feel something is not right. It can be the aura field of that home that has a lower level of energy than your own frequency.

When you live in such an aura field, you start feeling down and depressed. The more clutter and the more lack of light you have, the more you will feel uninspired and unhappy.

Surround Yourself with Pure Energy:

- You can place a white object in the West area of your living room, office, and bedroom
- Open yourself to new ideas: self-help and creativity books should be on your coffee table
- Place lights in all four corners of your living room and be sure there are no dark areas
- Avoid displaying broken objects
- Keep up with all home repairs
- Hang images of joy: like the sun, the beach, and flowers. Avoid hanging images of thunderstorms, ravines or images of winter in your home

- Open blinds to allow sunlight in your home
- Create a special place to meditate, pray or read

Extra Tips:

- Add lavender essential oil to your cleaning products
- Dust your furniture every week
- Remove any spider webs

Your Energy Journal

The Diamond Energy Principle of Transparency

"I Am Transparent in All I Do in the World"

4/ The Diamond Energy Principle of Transparency.

Transparency is the tenth Diamond Energy Principle and activates our health and wellbeing. You will learn how to activate this within you and in the space around you to attract 33.3% more health and wellbeing.

a/ Your Inner Activation of Transparency

To be able to manifest with speed, you need to make the aura field of your home transparent in order to see the gifts coming to you. How can you see what gifts the Universe is bringing if the air and the space around you are full of old energy?

The Law of Attraction can only really work if you live and work in an environment that is open to manifestation. When starting to clean up your inner self, it's hard to know how much you will need to clean up, but your home is a good reflection of the chaos inside of yourself.

If there is clutter and disorganization in your home, then I can guarantee that there are emotions and ideas that are blocked inside of you. By cleaning and decluttering the outside, your inside starts changing too.

Transparency is a constant focus, especially when several people live together in a home, use the same bathroom or work on the same computer. The more you create physical transparency in your home, the more you feel emotional, mental, and spiritual transparency and you will feel free of negative feelings, ideas, and vibrations.

When I feel blocked or feel that things are not moving how I want them to, I start cleaning up. I feel like I want to clean up my office, a closet, or my computer. It feels great to release old stuff and to create space for new gifts from the Universe.

When I was young, I loved to go inside old garages and storage places and throw everything out. Of course, I'd ask my family members what they wanted to keep. Turning a chaotic place into a place of order and beauty is still one of my favorite things to do!

During my life, I lived in many different countries and many homes. My favorite thing about moving is cleaning things up. Even if I don't move, I still get monthly urges to clean. If you do this regularly, your life keeps moving toward your goals. No goals can manifest when your environment is full of clutter and chaos.

A couple of students of mine asked me for advice. Their career was blocked. Everything was confusing to them. My students meditated and used all their knowledge about the Laws of the Universe, but nothing seemed to work. I offered them an hour of free Feng Shui consultation, but they had all kinds of excuses not to bring me to their home. One day I told them I was visiting no matter what. When I arrived, I saw that their home was so full of boxes that I could not even walk in the entrance without turning sideways!

They couldn't get to their bed or to their desk without literally climbing over these boxes. There was complete chaos and I understood why their wishes couldn't be fulfilled. There was no space to receive them and no transparency in their lives.

They didn't even know what was in the boxes or where things were. I urged them to release and to make their lives transparent. After taking three months to remove all the extra things in their apartment, new business opportunities were created, and they were able to finally get their lives back on track.

Diamond Energy Exercise

Take time to relax and close your eyes. Connect within by breathing consciously in and out. Then visualize yourself in a beautiful space in nature where you feel in complete harmony and peace. Imagine there is a quantum rainbow in the sky with 24 colors. You connect in with the ivory white aspect of this rainbow and fill your body and energy field with this color. From your head to your feet, you are filled with the ivory white energy of the Universe.

Focus now on your heart chakra in the center of your chest. As you breathe in, think about someone that you wish to be transparent with in your family, your friends or in the world. Radiate the ivory white color out from your heart chakra while you breathe out. Imagine that a ray of ivory white is reaching the heart of the person you are sending it to. You are radiating this color without expectations or judgments.

Say the following affirmation: ***"I Am Transparent with you."*** Focus again on the beautiful space around you in your visualization and open your eyes.

b/ The Diamond Energy Color of Transparency

The color of transparency is ivory white. It is said that elephants remember everything that happens in their lives, especially the negative experiences. An African Shaman once told me that everything is stored in their ivory teeth. The cleaner their teeth are, the less scars they have and the more they are free from negative vibrations.

How Can You Use This Color, Ivory White?

- You can place transparent glass items around and add flowers to transparent vases
- Place sea salt in the corners of every room of your home. If you leave it there for seven days, it will clear out any negative energetic vibrations

c/ Your Feng Shui Activation of Transparency.

When you are looking for something in your home and you can't find it easily, then your home is not transparent. The same goes with your computer or on your phone. If you need to find a file, a picture or an email and you can't find it in a couple of minutes, you have a lack of transparency.

When you have a problem in creating an organized and transparent home, you can connect with an organizer.

First, you can start with your office and make sure everything is filed properly. Next, make sure every room has its purpose. The dining room is for dining, and your bedroom is for sleeping. Avoid putting two purposes in one room, but if you need to, then make sure you divide the room. Let's say you have your desk in your bedroom. Make sure you place a dividing screen so that you don't see your bed while working and you do not see your desk while sleeping.

Surround Yourself with Transparency:

- Place a transparent item in the West area of your office or bedroom if you wish to create more transparency in your business or in your life
- The first impression people must have when they come into your home is orderly and clean energy
- Store all non-decorative items in boxes, drawers, or cabinets
- Discard expired food regularly

- Remove animal hair from your couch
- Keep books on shelves and tables
- Remove sick and old plants
- Take out the garbage before it overflows
- Be sure there is space around your desk
- Too much furniture in one space lacks transparency

Extra Tips:

- Open the windows every day to bring in fresh air
- Keep your pool and jacuzzi free of leaves and debris

Your Energy Journal

The Diamond Energy Principle of Forgiveness

"I Am Forgiveness in All I Was and All I Did"

5/ The Diamond Energy Principle of Forgiveness

Forgiveness is the eleventh Diamond Energy Principle and activates your health and wellbeing. You will learn how to activate this within you and in the space around you to attract 33.3% more health and wellbeing.

a/ Your Inner Activation of Forgiveness

In order to create new space and new opportunities for your life, you need to let go of the past. On an emotional level, we call this forgiveness. On a home level, we call this space clearing. When you're finding it hard to forgive yourself or others, I suggest you start by doing some space clearing.

The materials that surround you in your home and workspace include more than what you can see with the naked eye. It includes both matter and the aura field around it. It is in that aura field that those emotional vibrations are captured. Space clearing helps you to let go of objects connected with the past and the energy that you created in connection with them.

Perhaps you find it hard to let go of material around you. This is a little visualization that helps people clear the energy before they physically remove the things they no longer need. You can do an inner clearing by imagining that you are radiating violet energy from your heart and then send it out to the room you are in. Walk through the home and office, visualizing this violet vibration and clear each room.

When you start using the violet energy to let go of the past you will feel much more at ease. Perform this energetic space clearing each time you feel that your home feels old and stale.

You can even use the violet energy visualization in yourself. Simply visualize violet light coming from your feet and moving up toward your crown as it sweeps away everything with it that you wish to release.

Let it progress through your head and then give it back to the Universe, asking it to transform this old energy into good energy and send it back to you.

Diamond Energy Exercise

Take time to relax and close your eyes. Connect within by breathing consciously in and out. Then visualize yourself in a beautiful space in nature where you feel in complete harmony and peace. Imagine there is a quantum rainbow in the sky with 24 colors. You connect in with the violet aspect of this rainbow and fill your body and energy field with this color.

From your head to your feet, you are filled with the violet energy of the Universe. As you breathe in, you fill yourself with forgiveness and as you breathe out you are letting go of every thought, feeling and past action that limited your inner forgiveness.

After this you can connect with a situation, a goal or a relationship where you wish to have more forgiveness in and visualize the color Violet around and in it, until you feel the forgiveness is complete.

Say the following affirmation: ***"I Am Forgiveness in All I Was and in All I Did."*** Focus again on the beautiful space around you in your visualization and open your eyes.

b/ The Diamond Energy Color of Forgiveness

The color of forgiveness is violet. When we look at the rainbow, the highest color is violet and it's this color that vibrates the fastest on our planet.

When I first became a self-help teacher and a Feng Shui expert, I needed to let go of my career as a lawyer. I really needed to let go of the patterns that I created in that world. One day, when I needed a new car, I chose to buy a violet colored one to drive me to all of my classes and events. Each time I drove it, I imagined letting go of all the old patterns and behaviors in myself and with others. My students called it the Violet Flame car.

A great way to work with this color is to use the violet amethyst stone. Place an amethyst in the West area of your living room when you need to let go of emotional situations with your children and grandchildren.

Place it in the East area of your living room when you need to forgive your siblings. You can place it in the Southwest when you wish to forgive your mother. Place it in the Northwest when you wish to forgive your father. You can even place a little note under the stone explaining what you exactly wish to forgive.

How Can You Use This Color, Violet?

- Wear a violet outfit when you are asking for forgiveness or when you are forgiving
- Place an image of violets or place real violets in your home
- Burn violet candles when you pray for forgiveness
- Place a violet amethyst stone on your nightstand when you need to bring in some forgiveness in your personal romantic life

c/ Your Feng Shui Activation of Forgiveness

In order to receive new gifts from the Universe, you need to attract them in. However, if your space is full of old things that you previously attracted, then there is no space to receive anything new. A great way to start receiving again is by giving away. Giving away material connected with your old emotions and your old patterns stimulates forgiveness in you.

Every six months I do a space clearing of my closets and my possessions. When I let them go, I bless them, and I am grateful for what they meant in my life. I also know that others will be supported by these gifts.

Because I have moved many times in my life, I have become very good at letting go of things. The objects I choose to keep are attached to several special memories that I one day want to share with my kids. Try to keep one item from every period of your life because the stories behind them are more important than the items themselves.

Surround Yourself with Forgiveness:

- You can place a violet item in the Southeast
- Reduce your storage space to a minimum
- Bring bags with old clothes to Goodwill organizations
- Burn incense to help clean the air
- Organize a networking party with all new people
- Redecorate your home with new colors
- Practice space clearing techniques. For more information, check out my Diamond Space Clearing Online Program on my website
- Place bowls of sea saltwater in the corners of your rooms
- Free the entrance of your home from clutter

Extra Tips:

- The basement symbolizes the past, so if you need to store anything use the basement. Attics symbolize the future. Do not store the past in your attics. Do not keep storage under your bed or directly above it in the attic
- Do not keep things stored at your entrance, but rather at the back of your home

Your Energy Journal

The Diamond Energy Principle of Release

"I Release the Pain I Created in the World"

6/ The Diamond Energy Principle of Release

Release is the twelfth Diamond Energy Principle and activates your health and wellbeing. You will learn how to activate this within you and in the space around you to attract 33.3% more health and wellbeing.

a/ Your Inner Activation of Release

To create a brilliant future, you first need to do some release work. Every time you blame yourself and feel guilty for your past, you are stopping your brilliant future from happening. You can't keep moving forward with a backpack full of old "what ifs," "what could haves," and "what should haves." You can no longer change these events, but you can shift today by letting that emotional field be what it is: a great learning experience for yourself and perhaps for others.

When I teach people, they tell me that I have such great stories. Sure, they're entertaining stories now, but at one point they were events that were sometimes very hard and unpleasant. I could have kept them as rocks of guilt and blame that I carried in my backpack, but instead I decided to make stories from them and use them as gifts to others.

Letting go is easy when you know what is really happening in that process. Letting go is the short version of Letting God Be. Release is actually about letting God take care of you. You don't have to carry the burden anymore, neither in yourself nor in your home. God/the Universe will take care of it from now on.

The part of you that holds on to old energy is your ego. Your personality thinks that it's serving you best by holding onto things and memories. Tell your ego, "You know what; I think God/the Universe knows better."

Diamond Energy Exercise

Take time to relax and close your eyes. Connect within by breathing consciously in and out. Then visualize yourself in a beautiful space in nature where you feel in complete harmony and peace. Imagine there is a quantum rainbow in the sky with 24 colors. You connect in with the lilac aspect of this rainbow and fill your body and energy field with this color. From your head to your feet, you are filled with the lilac energy of the Universe.

Focus now on your heart chakra in the center of your chest. As you breathe in, think about someone or something that needs to be released from your family, your friends or in the world. Radiate the lilac color out from your heart chakra while you breathe out. Imagine that a ray of lilac is reaching the heart of the person you are sending it to. You are radiating this color, without expectations or judgments.

Say the following affirmation: ***"I Release for you."*** Focus again on the beautiful space around you in your visualization and open your eyes.

b/ The Diamond Energy Color of Release

The color of release is lilac. Lilac is the color of the lavender flower, which was used by many of our grandmothers. They placed little bags with dried lavender flowers in closets. The smell of lavender helps us to be in the moment and to no longer feel stuck in the past.
I love lavender mist or anything else with that essence. It makes me feel both happy and present in the moment. When I need to release something on an emotional level, I put lavender essential oil on my hands, smell it, and then wave it around my body in my aura field. I always feel relaxed after using it.

When I need to deal with letting go of papers, files or clothes, I will always spray some lavender mist. I even have lavender oil with me when I travel and need to sleep in a hotel room. You never know what happens in unfamiliar places and so you will want to release any unwanted energy.

I wave some lavender energy around, especially in the corners of a room since this is where the negative energy gets piled up the most. Also put some drops of lavender essential oil on your pillow and you will be able to let go of your busy day and find a restful sleep.

How Can You Use This Color, Lilac?

- Buy some small lavender bags and put them in your closets
- When you have a hard time letting go of people and memories, wear lilac outfits
- Spread lavender mist in your living room; it will help you enjoy the day

c/ Your Feng Shui Activation of Release.

Your home is a reflection of your life. When you have built up shame in yourself, it will seem that you are ashamed of your home. You will have created so much chaos that you don't dare invite others in.

When you have built up a lot of guilt, you will have piles of old books, magazines and papers. You feel guilty about letting go of something because you never know when you can use it someday.

Surround Yourself with Releasing Power:

- Place lavender flowers or a lilac item in the Southeast of a bedroom or an office
- Go through your boxes with pictures and decide which ones you wish to keep and then put them in photo albums. Give

them a place in your personal success direction or in the East section of your living room to enhance the family energy

- Release the old energy in your home by burning sandalwood incense
- Remove burial masks from your home
- Replace pictures of your former partner
- Hang the most current pictures of your children and grandchildren. Don't hang images of their baby years if they are over twenty years old.
- Remove anything that connects you with a bad experience or relationship so you can let it go
- Return books, DVDs, CD's, and clothes to the person whom you are no longer associated with
- When a person passes away, take your time to release their belongings. Do not put images of people that passed on in your bedroom. You can place them in your living space

Extra Tips:

- Invite some friends to create a Release party. It is more fun with others and you will be more motivated to remove things
- Read your letters one more time, listen to the music one more time, or put on that dress one more time and then bless them and let them go

Your Energy Journal

C. Energize your Relationships.

To help enhance your personal and professional relationships there are six Diamond Energy Principles that you can activate. These principles are:

- Love
- Tenderness
- Balance
- Passion
- Harmony
- Collaboration

You will encounter details about these principles in the next chapter.

The Diamond Energy Principle of Love

"I Am Love in All
I Am and All I Do"

1/ The Diamond Energy Principle of Love.

Love is the thirteenth Diamond Energy Principle and activate all your relationships. You will learn how to activate this within you and in the space around you to attract 33.3% more wonderful Relationships.

a/ Your Inner Activation of Love

The word "Love" and the word "Law" are derived from the same origin. The Law of the Universe is love. And it starts with you. Do you love yourself? I am not speaking about adoring what you wear or what you look like but whether you love who you are? What you are doing? The life that you created? When you give love to yourself, you will start receiving love from others. Love is a flow of energy. When you want it to appear in your life, you better start sharing it with yourself and others.

Start loving yourself and others will fall in love with you, too. You can't expect your romantic partner to love you if you don't love being their husband or wife. You can't expect your friends to love you when you don't love being their friends. So, start loving by placing images in your home that reflect love. Use items that symbolically express the quality of love in yourself and in others.

When I was eighteen years old, I had a wonderful relationship, but after that one summer, for several years, I didn't attract a boyfriend. I had many friends, but not one romance. My friends told me many times that I was blind because I didn't see that men were interested in me.

Interestingly enough, I started drawing more intensely when I was eighteen years old and the image I drew over and over again was of a woman with one eye. The other eye was covered by long hair. I created a series of these portraits and called them 'The Muses.' I hung them above my bed and, indeed, I attracted many slumber parties with my friends, but no boyfriend. I basically said to the Universe I wanted to be surrounded by girlfriends. I had not drawn one image of a couple.

In addition, I had mirrors across my bed which doubled my solitude. Although I knew about Feng Shui, I didn't understand all of the consequences yet. When I was twenty-six years old, I replaced them with images of couples and about six months later I found my husband with whom I am still happily married.

Diamond Energy Exercise

Take time to relax and close your eyes. Connect within by breathing consciously in and out. Then visualize yourself in a beautiful space in nature where you feel in complete harmony and peace. Imagine there is a quantum rainbow in the sky with 24 colors. You connect in with the rose aspect of this rainbow and fill your body and energy field with this color.

From your head to your feet, you are filled with the rose energy of the Universe. As you breathe in, you fill yourself with love and as you breathe out you are letting go of every thought, feeling and past action that limited your inner love.

After this you can connect with a situation, a goal or a relationship where you wish to have more love and visualize the color rose around and in it until you feel it is completely love.

Say the following affirmation: ***"I Am Love in All I Am and in All I Do."*** Focus again on the beautiful space around you in your visualization and open your eyes.

b/ The Diamond Energy Color of Love

The color of love is rose. I am sure it is no surprise to anyone, especially since that is the name of the flower most associated with Valentine's Day.

How Can You Use the Color, Rose?

- When you have a meeting with a loved one, give them a rose. Love will be in the air, guaranteed!
- Place rose flowers in your garden at the entrance so everyone will feel welcomed and loved even before they walk into your home.
- If you haven't had enough love in the air, start spreading rose mist or use a rose flower essential oil in your bath to attract love.

c/ Your Feng Shui Activation of Love

Love is in the air. In certain homes, you feel the love hanging around. You don't want to leave that place because the whole atmosphere breathes love. The smell, the colors, the coziness, and the warmth of the people are welcoming to you.

Even in a shop or an office, love can be in the air. If you have ever walked into a shop where the people hate what they sell, you probably didn't return. But if you enter shops where they love their products and are happy to sell them to you, you will want to come back again.

When you enter your own home or office, you need to feel the love in the air. If you don't, then do not be surprised if you are unable to attract lovely relationships, customers or clients.

Like I said, you need to have love for yourself first and foremost. You also need to activate love in the relationships with your past or current family.

Love in your romantic relationships is of course something that people dream about. Where is the princess that I need to rescue from the dragon? Where is the prince on the white horse? If your tower is not ready, your prince will not come. You can also attract more general loving relationships that will support you, like good friends. Giving love and receiving love from your children and grandchildren is always a part of a loving life.

Surround Yourself with Loving Energy:

When you come into your home:

- Place a rose colored item in the Southwest area of your bedroom, office, or living room to attract more love in your life
- Place pictures of you and your family in your living room. Make sure you are in the picture
- Hang drawings from your children or grandchildren and provide a box with toys for young ones to play with
- Let images of romantic couples or your own wedding pictures have a central place in the living room and bedroom. Above your headboard or opposite the bed when you wake up are the best places. Also place a personal romantic picture in your personal relationship direction.
- Items are in pairs to send the message of positive relationships
- Hang up a team picture in your office
- Place a couple of rose quartz stone hearts in the Southwest of your bedroom
- Add the Chinese double happiness symbol in the Southwest of your living room

Activate Your Personal Romantic Relationships

Place in the Southwest of your bedroom and living room a symbol, a book, or an image that represents your personal relationship.

Activate Your Relationship with Your Children and Grandchildren

Place in the West of your living or family room the pictures, drawings, or toys of your small ones. You can place ornaments related to the children, or an image of children playing.

Activate Your Relationship with Your Friends

Place in the Northwest of your living room, images of you and your friends, your address book, or a statue of a friendship circle.

Activate Your Relationships with Your Family

Place in the East of your living room or family room, images of your family. A family symbol, like a family tree, can be as effective.

Activate your Personal Relationship Direction.

You can also place personal images of your relationships, especially the ones that can use some extra care, position them in your Personal Relationship direction.

Extra Tips:

- Always travel with pictures of your loved ones
- Place an image of the people who live with you at the entrance, showing them each time they enter the home that they are welcome. Make sure you are in the picture with them
- If you wish to never be alone in your life, make sure you are always with others in pictures

Your Energy Journal

The Diamond Energy Principle of Tenderness

"I Take Care with Tenderness of All That Is in the World"

2/ The Diamond Energy Principle of Tenderness

Tenderness is the fourteenth Diamond Energy Principle and activates all your relationships. You will learn how to activate this within you and in the space around you to attract 33.3% more wonderful relationships.

a/ Your Inner Activation of Tenderness.

When I listen to "Love Me Tender," the famous song by Elvis Presley, I always feel so tender in my heart. Sweet voices can really touch me. But what makes us feel tender differs for all of us.

Even if you are a man, you can bring tenderness. If the king of rock and roll was allowed to be tender, then so are all men. This song changed something in the consciousness of the Western world.

You need to take time to bring tenderness into your body, your mind, and your soul. Numerous products and treatments are out there to help you bring tenderness to your physical body. But, let's be honest, the mind is oversaturated with constant information and technical gadgets that tend to override your need for tenderness. Tenderness is sometimes hidden in the silence between these pieces of information. Less is definitely more when you wish to be tender to yourself.

Be sure to receive and share tender gestures and words with others. Let your eyes see sweet and tender images. Let your nose smell sweet scents. Let your ears hear harmonious sounds and voices.

When I am on a holiday or on a weekend trip, I really focus on being tender to myself. It will start by going to a great hotel where they have smooth carpets to walk on and linens that smell nice and feel soft. Maybe there will be a view from the balcony that overlooks a beautiful valley or the ocean.

I will seek out a wonderful restaurant where I can smell all the delicious food prepared by a great chef and brought by a waiter who knows their job. Luxury can feel like tenderness to me.

After that, my body is satisfied and I am ready to let my soul feel the tenderness of the Universe by walking in nature and being in the company of my family.

One luxurious version of tenderness I experienced was when I was invited on one of the largest yachts in St. Tropez in the South of France. My senses felt incredibly satisfied: we had great food and were surrounded by the beauty of the ocean.

But a week later I was invited to an apartment of a friend near Mont Blanc. Unfortunately, it was the opposite of beauty in her home. It was a typical French apartment, and although she was very welcoming, the smell and the greyness of her walls was a shock to my senses, especially in contrast to the heightened tenderness I had just experienced. However, the way she welcomed me and my family felt very tender to my heart.

I decided to go for a hike in the mountains to touch base with the tenderness of nature. I ended up in a bad storm and slept at a farm. The welcoming farmer's family gave me bread and fresh cheese, a warm fire and a place to sleep in the hay above the cows. The cats warmed me up and protected me from the rats and mice.

That night my heart was full of true tenderness for this family, for nature, and for all of nature's scents. Walking down the mountain after a fresh storm, my senses were the clearest they had ever been. I felt touched by the tenderness of the Universe in me and around me.

Diamond Energy Exercise

Take time to relax and close your eyes. Connect within by breathing consciously in and out. Then visualize yourself in a beautiful space in nature where you feel in complete harmony and peace. Imagine there is a quantum rainbow in the sky with 24 colors. You connect in with the pink aspect of this rainbow and fill your body and energy field with this color. From your head to your feet, you are filled with the pink energy of the Universe.

Focus now on your heart chakra in the center of your chest. As you breathe in, think about someone that you need to be more tender to in your family, your friends or in the world. Radiate the pink color out from your heart chakra while you breathe out. Imagine that a ray of pink is reaching the heart of the person you are sending it to. You are radiating this color without expectations or judgments.

Say the following affirmation: ***"I treat you with Tenderness."*** Focus again on the beautiful space around you in your visualization and open your eyes.

b/ The Diamond Energy Color of Tenderness

The color of tenderness is pink. When babies are born, we know that touching their skin is such a tender feeling. It has a pink color, unlike anything else. That kind of tenderness is evoked when we bring pink into our lives.

After a period of wearing a lot of dark colors for my career as a lawyer, I longed to wear pink. I bought everything in this color. Actually, while writing this chapter, I'm wearing a pink outfit with the sound of the fountain outside and the melody of a wind chime. I feel like I am in heaven.

How Can You Use This Color, Pink?

- Wear a pink underwear, a pink nightgown, or a pink shirt (even a pink shirt for men) this will bring forward the tender aspect of yourself
- Place a bouquet of pink roses on your dining room table
- You can also hang images of pink flowers in the hallways leading to your bedroom.

c/ Your Feng Shui Activation of Tenderness

A home is like your second womb. When you were inside the womb, the water was the right temperature to give you comfort, and the voice of your mother and the contact of her hands on her belly gave you a tender feeling. When you take a warm bath, you subconsciously remember that feeling and when you have a massage this deepest memory of relaxation comes back.

Surround Yourself with Tender Energy.

- Place a pink item in the Southwest area of your bedroom.
- Place items in pairs, like two hearts, two candles, an image of a couple.
- Hang up images of angels
- Use soft and sensuous fabrics on your bed
- Have pillows in pastel colors or in heart forms
- Have a warm and soft carpet next to your bed when you wake up
- Make sure you alarm clock plays soft music when you wake up
- Cover your mirrors in your bedroom as it stops tender intimacy between a couple
- Hang up images of smiling people around you
- Hang up a wind chime to provide a tender background sound
- Place a birdbath and/or a bird feeder in your garden

- Have a bubbling fountain that provides soothing sounds. The best place for a fountain is in the Southeast or the North area of your living room. office or garden
- Hang crystals on your windows and watch as they reflect the intense sunlight, creating rainbows

Extra Tips:

- Place images of fairies, gnomes, dragonflies or butterflies in your garden
- Place stuffed animals around you or on your bed

Your Energy Journal

The Diamond Energy Principle of Balance

"I Am Balance in All I Am And in All I Do"

3/ The Diamond Energy Principle of Balance

Balance is the fifteenth Diamond Energy Principle and activates all your relationships. You will learn how to activate this within you and in the space around you to attract 33.3% more wonderful relationships.

a/ Your Inner Activation of Balance

When you ask the Universe for success, energy, passionate relationships, and unlimited inspiration, you are in for a surprise. The Universe balances things out.

There are, in fact, times when the Universe gives you nothing but down time. It does this to prepare you for the next possible level. The Universe knows exactly what you need to attain your goals. When nothing happens, know that it is part of the manifestation but perhaps you need to balance some things out before you can receive. Balance is the platform where long-term relationships can become successful. Balance in a relationship is about finding a perfect unity between:

- Time together and time spending by yourself alone
- Passion and tenderness
- Wild partying and walking by the sea
- Playing with your children and having intimate dinners with your partner
- Laughter and fun and deep conversations
- Staying at home and going outside in nature

You need to take care of this principle if you feel that there is no balance between your inside and outside life experiences. When you tend to create conflict with others, it would be best to focus on balance.

If you have mood swings that affect your relationships, if you are excessively stubborn, or if you find that you cannot talk peacefully with your partner, then focus on balance to set things right.

When I came to live in the United States of America, I didn't have a lot of furniture for my family. Being a first generation immigrant and trying to make my dreams come true created a lot of stress for me. Many times, my family and I were ready to stop the adventure and go back home.

There were times when we experienced lack of cash flow and we didn't have enough money for food and clothing. During that time, a couple of friends gave us a couple of ruby red couches. I always felt that the fact that they were ruby red and big created a balance for my family.

Diamond Energy Exercise

Take time to relax and close your eyes. Connect within by breathing consciously in and out. Then visualize yourself in a beautiful space in nature where you feel in complete harmony and peace. Imagine there is a quantum rainbow in the sky with 24 colors. You connect in with the ruby red aspect of this rainbow and fill your body and energy field with this color.

From your head to your feet, you are filled with the ruby red energy of the Universe. As you breathe in, you fill yourself with balance and as you breathe out you are letting go of every thought, feeling and past action that limited your inner balance.

After this you can connect with a situation, a goal or a relationship where you wish to have more balance in and visualize the color ruby red around and in it, until you feel it is completely in balance.

Say the following affirmation: ***"I Am Balance in All I Am and in All I Do."*** Focus again on the beautiful space around you in your visualization and open your eyes.

b/ The Diamond Energy Color of Balance

The color of balance is ruby red. Ruby is a gemstone that helps create Balance in your life. The deep red color is sometimes used to balance the white of the yang energy and the black of the yin energy. That is why the combination of red, white, and black is often so popular.

How Can You Use This Color, Ruby Red?

- Place ruby red placemats on the table to create balance in your family
- Give the woman in your life jewelry with a ruby gemstone to help her balance her life

c/ Your Feng Sui activation of Balance

When there is too much furniture, too many paintings and too many different colors in your home, your senses cannot find balance. Sometimes less is more!

For instance, although I love to work with colors, I only have one color that is consistent throughout every room. For me, gold is the color: sometimes in pillows, in ornaments or in curtains.

Choose any color that feels good for you. Make sure one room is not empty and another is full of furniture. Make sure you can easily pass around all of the furniture, and that when you look at a room, it makes you feel content.

Surround Yourself with Balancing Energy.

- Place a ruby red item in the South area of your office or bedroom
- Place a yin yang symbol in the center of your home.
- Place ruby red items in your interior design.
- Place all five elements in your environment: water, wood, fire, earth, and metal
- When you live in an L-shaped, U-shaped or T-shaped home: balance it with lights and adding patios or gardens to make it a square or rectangular form
- Avoid placing anything higher than eye level on boards or on cabinets
- Have everything in couples or in even numbers: like 2, 4, or 6 chairs
- Avoid having a staircase or a bathroom in the center of your home
- Make sure carpets and rugs are neat and even so you don't trip
- Avoid towering books in such a way that they could fall
- Store toys and clothing properly and avoid having them on the ground

Extra Tips:

- Don't put water and fire together or you create a clash of imbalance
- Make sure your fridge is filled with balanced foods like vegetables and fruits

Your Energy Journal

The Diamond Energy Principle of Passion

"I Am Passionate in What I Do For the World"

4/ The Diamond Energy Principle of Passion.

Passion is the sixteenth Diamond Energy Principle and activates all your relationships. You will learn how to activate this within you and in the space around you to attract 33.3% more wonderful relationships.

a/ Your Inner Activation of Passion

Passion is the fuel that makes your dreams come to life. Successful people are passionate about what they do. This is why they attract the right partners and clients.

Passion attracts. If you look at people who succeed it is not only because they are good at what they do, but it is also that they have passion for making their dreams come true.

Do You Want It Passionately Enough?

Live your life from the standpoint that every day can be your last. You don't have to think it is definitely your last but live your life with the passion of having this one chance to succeed *today*.

Every relationship needs passion in it, but before it can be there, you need to be passionate about yourself and about your life in general. Most relationships end because there is no passion in the lives of the couple. Although most people think that sexual passion is what counts the most, it's a couple's ability to relate to each other in a passionate way that is the basis for success.

Find your common passions. You can share your passion for your children, you can be passionate about music or a rock band. You can be passionate about serving the community or the church or about supporting your local basketball team.

Most couples sit in front of the TV after their workday and have no passion in their lives. They can stick together, but with what result? Life has been passing by instead of being lived.

When you are passionate about something, it will be easier to manifest. If you are not passionate about your love for someone then your relationship is less likely to succeed. I often see only one person in a couple that is passionately in love with the other. Sure, the other partner is in love, but they don't believe it with every cell in their body.

Passion is about knowing that you are meant for each other in every cell of your existence. That is why when someone falls in love and there is some resistance toward their relationship from their families, passion can kick in and they will try to make it work in a way that others could never imagine.

When I met my husband, there was a great deal of resistance toward him from my friends (because I had a college degree and he only went to school until he was fifteen), from my family (because he was divorced and had a four-year-old child), but their resistance made me aware of my soul passion for him.

Now we have been together for more than twenty five years and we have a passionate relationship. Whilst I am still very passionate about living my true passion, transforming the world, we do share several mutual passions: our children, our dogs, music, and enjoying a good and healthy life.

When you are passionate it doesn't mean that you won't clash with each other occasionally, but it does mean that you have a passionate foundation to fall back on after clashing.

Diamond Energy Exercise

Take time to relax and close your eyes. Connect within by breathing consciously in and out. Then visualize yourself in a beautiful space in nature where you feel in complete harmony and peace. Imagine there is a quantum rainbow in the sky with 24 colors. You connect in with the cherry red aspect of this rainbow and fill your body and energy field with this color. From your head to your feet, you are filled with the cherry red energy of the Universe.

Focus now on your heart chakra in the center of your chest. As you breathe in, think about someone who you wish to send more passion to in your family, your friends or in the world. Radiate the cherry red color out from your heart chakra while you breathe out. Imagine that a ray of cherry red is reaching the heart of the person you are sending it to. You are radiating this color without expectations or judgments.

Say the following affirmation: ***"I create Passion for You."*** Focus again on the beautiful space around you in your visualization and open your eyes.

b/ The Diamond Energy Color of Passion

The color of passion is cherry red. Have you seen a young couple in love eating ripe cherries together? Cherries come in pairs and ought to be eaten as a couple. In fact, cherries are a symbol of passion. In the movie "The Secret", I was wearing a cherry red shirt. After two hours of interviewing, Rhonda Byrne told me that I would be in the movie because I am so passionate about what I share. I smiled; the cherry red had its effect! I always wear colors with a purpose, and that day I knew I had to do something special to show my passion for this movie.

How Can You Use This Color, Cherry Red?

- Place cherry red napkins or candles when you have an intimate dinner with your partner
- Place images of your loved ones in a cherry red frame
- Wear a cherry red outfit when you want to give a passionate speech or when you want to attract passionate people

c/ Your Feng Shui Activation of Passion

Although I have a passion for colors and beauty, I sometimes see that others seem satisfied living in a home without colors and beauty. The word "passion" first meant suffering and misery (as in the Passion of Christ, or of a martyr) before it changed into the meaning of having strong desire or emotion. That is why people still think when you are passionate about something or someone that you will suffer.

It wasn't until the 16th century that the word picked up the meaning of having a strong enthusiasm and liking for something. In this century, we really need to embrace the most recent meaning over the original.

Allow your life to represent your passion. If you are passionate about cars, then make sure they are represented as images and statues in your home. If you are passionate about your children, then place their pictures around you in the right places according to Feng Shui. I always ask people what their passion is, and then I ask how it shows up in their environment.

Surround Yourself with Passionate Energy:

- Place a cherry red item or an image of cherries in the South area of your bedroom or living room.
- Put out images and statues of the things or people you are passionate about.

- Include cherry red colors in your interior design.
- Display images or statues that reflect passion in your bedroom.
- Place a bouquet of red roses in your dining room.
- Use colored placemats, napkins, candles, and pillows to spice up your interior.
- Place aromatic candles in your living spaces.

Extra Tips:

- Don't hang up too many images of water because they cool down the passion in your life, especially in your bedroom
- Don't hang romantic images of family pictures on the door of your fridge. You are freezing your relationships and the passion you have for people

Your Energy Journal

The Diamond Energy Principle of Harmony

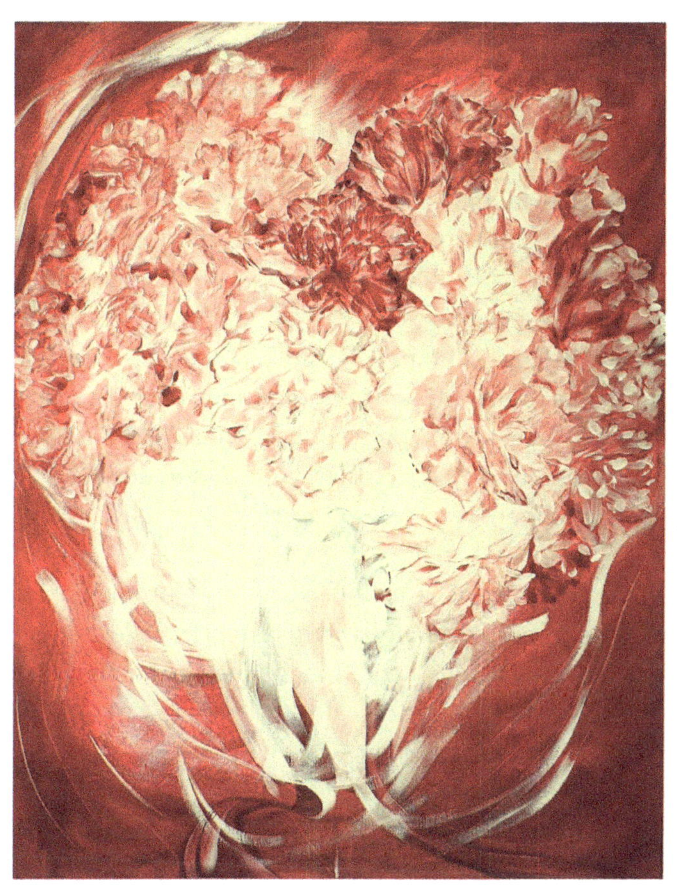

"I Am Peaceful in All I Am And in All I Do"

5/ The Diamond Energy Principle of Harmony

Harmony is the seventeenth Diamond Energy Principle and activates all your relationships. You will learn how to activate this within you and in the space around you to attract 33.3% more wonderful relationships.

a/ Your Inner Activation of Harmony

What is harmony? It is the moment in your life that you are simply happy, for no special reason. You are just *happy*. Nothing spectacular may be happening, but you are nonetheless in harmony between the heavenly and the earthly energy. It is about feeling content.

Of course, life has its moments of drama. Sometimes you witness the drama of others and it influences your inner harmony. It would be good to have an image you can immediately go to when you experience outside stress, so that your inner self taps into that harmonious moment.

You are a real Master of Transformation in relationships when you can remain peaceful in the midst of disaster. In order to do this, you need to practice by taking some inner time for harmony on a daily basis.

When I was a young girl, there were many conflicts in my home, especially when my older siblings came home and my parents argued with them about their lives, long hair, politics, often until the early morning in the family room which was situated just under my bedroom.

So, the only thing for me to do was to leave that room and sit on the top of the chair, praying to the Divine Mother Mary. I was raised Catholic and she was the saint who represented harmony for me. I also visualized, between the shouting and yelling, a place of harmony which for me was my tree house. If they were arguing during the day, I went high up the tree, experiencing the harmony of nature around me.

Even at night, I went there in my mind. The background noise disappeared, and I survived those years.

Diamond Energy Exercise

Take time to relax and close your eyes. Connect within by breathing consciously in and out. Then visualize you are in a beautiful space in nature where you feel in complete harmony and peace. Imagine there is a quantum rainbow in the sky with 24 colors. You connect in with the magenta aspect of this rainbow and fill your body and energy field with this color.

From your head to your feet, you are filled with the magenta energy of the Universe. As you breathe in, you fill yourself with harmony and as you breathe out you are letting go of every thought, feeling and past action that limited your inner harmony.

After this you can connect with a situation, a goal or a relationship where you wish to have more inner harmony and visualize the color magenta around and in it until you feel it is completely in harmony.

Say the following affirmation: ***"I Am Harmony in All I Am and in All I Do."*** Focus again on the beautiful space around you in your visualization and open your eyes.

b/ The Diamond Energy Color of Harmony

The color of harmony is magenta. This color is equal parts red and blue. The name for the color originated after the 1859 battle of Magenta in Italy when harmony returned to that region.

When you need to go to a space or a situation that is very emotional, you can wear magenta. When I have just received bad news, like perhaps I need to visit a loved one in the hospital, I make sure I have a gift with a magenta ribbon.

How Can You Use This Color, Magenta?

- You can wear magenta when you need to be in an environment that has emotional and dramatic energy
- Have a magenta candle that you can light after a conflict in your home
- Add some magenta accessories to your children's outfits so they stay calm and harmonious and don't attract bullies

c/ Your Feng Shui Activation of Harmony

Have you ever sat down on a warm rock near a river at the end of a summer day? The smell of the flowers surrounds you and you feel the breeze in your hair. This is a time when you have all the five elements present: the warm rock (earth), the river (water), the sun (fire), the flowers (wood), and the breeze (metal).

That is exactly how your home should feel when it is in perfect harmony. Harmony creates inspiration, and when you are in that energy field you have access to the information that the Universe is sending back to you in response to your requests.

Surround Yourself With Harmonious Energy:

- Place magenta in the Northeast area of your living room
- Burn candles to relax the atmosphere
- Play soft, harmonious background music
- Serve tea and cookies to your guests
- Remove any images of war or conflict
- Provide soft pillows, couches and towels
- Be sure your home has a sweet scent

Extra Tips:

- Order creates harmony. Let your family know when you will all be eating and when you will arrive home
- Try to make family time and make sure that your work stays outside of the family room

Your Energy Journal

The Diamond Energy Principle of Collaboration

"I Collaborate with Others to Create a Better World"

6/ The Diamond Energy Principle of Collaboration.

Collaboration is the eighteenth Diamond Energy Principle to activate your relationships. You will learn how to activate this within you and in the space around you to attract 33.3% more wonderful relationships.

a/ Your Inner Activation of Collaboration.

You are responsible for every thought, feeling, or action that you take. But this 100% responsibility doesn't mean you can't share your workload with others. You can do your journey alone, but it is much more fun to team up with others!

After the movie 'The Secret: came out, people started to come together spontaneously to watch the movie and to implement the knowledge that had been shared. The movie itself showed collaboration between teachers, and was a new way of teaching self-help information.

Collaboration is finding a win-win situation in your relationships with others. It is about sharing your accomplishments with your team. Collaboration is feeling free to share a new idea with others so you can team up with them. Collaboration with like-minded people can totally change the world.

For a long time in my youth, I felt very lonely. I wanted to speak about my spiritual experiences and what I already knew about Transformation. But with my friends, I had to hold back and instead talk about boys and fashion.

I didn't attract friends that thought like me. It just so happened that I was more spiritually mature than most of my friends. I thought about the big questions of life and had many spiritual "aha!" experiences.

I remember that I wanted to have the experience of like-minded or like-souled friends. I started writing with a fuchsia-colored pen to people I already knew hoping that I would find someone who would have a soul collaboration with me. I started going to a youth movement where I slowly began connecting with people who wrote poetry and who were very artistic and creative.

With my new friends, we started collaborating in creating theatres and musicals for children's events. For the first time, I felt what collaboration could do in my life in terms of being on the same level of awareness with others. I chose, and still choose, of course, fuchsia in shawls and outfits to celebrate the nature of collaboration.

Diamond Energy Exercise

Take time to relax and close your eyes. Connect within by breathing consciously in and out. Then visualize yourself in a beautiful space in nature where you feel in complete harmony and peace. Imagine there is a quantum rainbow in the sky with 24 colors. You connect in with the fuchsia aspect of this rainbow and fill your body and energy field with this color. From your head to your feet, you are filled with the fuchsia energy of the Universe.

Focus now on your heart chakra in the center of your chest. As you breathe in, think about someone that you wish to collaborate better with in your family, your friends or in the world. Radiate the fuchsia color out from your heart chakra while you breathe out. Imagine that a ray of fuchsia is reaching the heart of the person you are sending it to. You are radiating this color without expectations or judgments.

Say the following affirmation: ***"I Am in Collaboration with you."*** Focus again on the beautiful space around you in your visualization and open your eyes.

b/ The Diamond Energy Color of Collaboration

The color of collaboration is fuchsia. Fuchsia, along with orange, was one of the colors most used in the United States in the sixties and seventies during the Flower Power era. The two colors represented celebration and collaboration. The term, a win-win situation, is definitely connected with the hippy movement. "You do something for me, brother and I do something for you, sister."

How Can You Use This Color, Fuchsia?

- Place a fuchsia candle in front of your team picture
- Place fuchsia-colored flowers in a team meeting room

c/ Your Feng Shui Activation for Collaboration

When people put out images of a person alone, they are not only promoting lack of romance but also a lack of collaboration. They show that you are trying to do things by yourself. The Universe will obey this request. But you can also show the Universe that, in your home, it will be fun doing things as a team or with friends and family.

Surround Yourself with Collaborative Energy:

- Place a fuchsia item in the Southwest of your office or living room
- Place a picture of you with your whole family
- Place pictures out at the entrance of your business and management team, or of the board of directors.
- Put up the logos of the companies that you collaborate with, or put banners of them on your website
- Place an image of you and your mentors on your desk
- Remove any images of fierce animals attacking each other
- Place images of your memberships

Extra Tips:

- When you don't like to put up personal pictures, find images of team sports where collaboration means creating victory, like rowing or sailing a boat together
- You can also place a friendship circle in ceramic to enforce the energy of working together

Your Energy Journal

D. Energize your Wisdom

To help enhance your knowledge, wisdom, Intuition and Inspiration, and your spiritual connection with God/Universe, there are six Diamond Energy Principles that you can activate. These principles are:

- Wisdom
- Compassion
- Clarity
- Focus
- Transformation
- Faith

You will encounter details about these principles in the next chapter.

The Diamond Energy Principle of Wisdom

"I Am Wisdom in All I Am and All I Do"

1/ The Diamond Energy Principle of Wisdom

Wisdom is the nineteenth Diamond Energy Principle and activates your knowledge and inspiration. You will learn how to activate this within you and in the space around you to attract 33.3% more wisdom.

a/ Your Inner Activation of Wisdom

Wisdom is the combination of intuition, inspiration, and knowledge. True wisdom is one of the greatest riches you could ever receive. It cannot be measured financially; it's priceless. In addition to the Universe providing for you wealth, happiness, and great health, it also provides you with all of the wisdom you need in your life to make the right decisions, to have discernment, and to know what your next steps on your Transformational journey are.

In your busy life, you need to stop for five minutes and ask yourself if you have a problem. It is only when you are aware you have a stressful situation that you can really start taking steps towards change. But sometimes we don't have enough information and knowledge to know what the next steps are.

This principle is also about your spiritual or religious life. Transformation is not connected with any religion, culture or race.

Instead, it is a way of life that connects you with every religion, spiritual practice, culture or race. Whatever you wish to attract, it is your responsibility and your decision. No one has the right to express any judgments about what you wish to attract in order to grow spiritually and about your spiritual practice in your life.

Successful people are and remain students of life. You know that you will never know everything. The more you know, the more you know there is still so much you do not know. Success comes when you have the right attitude about yourself in regard to wisdom, and by allowing wisdom to be displayed and attracted in your home and office.

Therefore, it is important to feel inspired every day and to find ways of inspiration by reading books, by meditating, and listening to seminars in person or online. We are in a time cycle of human experience where knowledge and wisdom are the keys for creating wealth. This cycle started in 2004 and will last until 2024. The greatest wealth you can experience is sharing your wisdom and knowledge to improve the lives of millions.

One of the most fulfilling things about being a teacher is to receive emails from people where they share how they were inspired by you or how your wisdom has changed their lives. I will always tell them that now it is their turn to share. True wisdom is not meant for one person, but is shared with family, friends, and anyone seeking wisdom.

When "The Secret" DVD came out, I took one DVD with me on an airplane from Minneapolis to Los Angeles. I told myself that the person who ended up sitting next to me would receive the DVD. I played a little game with the Universe and changed my seats when checking in.

When I arrived at my seat, I put the DVD in the back pocket of the seat in front of me and a young man soon sat down next to me and started reading a book about life insurance. I am sure it contained valuable information, but perhaps it was a little boring because he stopped reading after fifteen minutes.

Then I asked him what he would do the next morning. He looked at me, startled by this strange question, and he shared that he just returned from a financial seminar with his mentor, who told him to order the DVD "The Secret" in the morning. I told him that he wouldn't need to order it. The man looked completely surprised.

I took the DVD out of the pocket in front of me and gave it to him. He almost yelled, "Wow! This stuff really works!" I immediately asked him what else his mentor told him to do. He said he was told to attend a seminar with one of the teachers featured in the DVD in the coming months because it would be very beneficial for him. I smiled, introduced myself as Marie Diamond, one of the teachers in the movie, and told him he had three hours to ask me any questions he needed answers for. This young man was seeking wisdom.

After three hours, the man was in tears from all the wisdom he received. He asked me what he could do to repay me for my time. I said that God/the Universe gave him some free time with me, but that he could repay it by sharing the Wisdom with his family and friends. I suggested getting the DVD anyway and giving it to a friend or family member.

Diamond Energy Exercise

Take time to relax and close your eyes. Connect within by breathing consciously in and out. Then visualize yourself in a beautiful space in nature where you feel in complete harmony and peace. Imagine there is a quantum rainbow in the sky with 24 colors. You connect in with the yellow aspect of this rainbow and fill your body and energy field with this color.

From your head to your feet, you are filled with the yellow energy of the Universe. As you breathe in, you fill yourself with wisdom and as you breathe out you are letting go of every thought, feeling and past action that limited your inner wisdom.

After this you can connect with a situation, a goal or a relationship where you wish to have more wisdom in and visualize the color yellow around and in it, until you feel it is completely filled with wisdom.

Say the following affirmation: ***"I Am Wisdom in All I Am and in All I Do."*** Focus again on the beautiful space around you in your visualization and open your eyes.

b/ The Diamond Energy Color of Wisdom

The color of wisdom is yellow. The warm yellow of the sunlight brings us insights and wisdom. Yellow is a great color to have around you. It is one of my favorite colors to use in interior designs, especially in the rooms of children and teenagers. They will grow up to be wise young people.

How Can You Use This Color, Yellow?

- Place yellow flowers on your coffee table so that everyone in the home or office will act wisely in their communications
- Wear this color in your outfit as an accessory if you feel you need to support your inner wisdom

c/ Your Feng Shui Activation of Wisdom

A home is like a temple for your Soul, but it does not need to look like a temple. Only if you wish to live as a monk or not to have any physical intimacy would I suggest making a temple of your home!

However, there still needs to be a place or certain areas that give you peace and inspiration. A person cannot live from money and love alone. You need time and a place to recharge your inner batteries. You need to let the Universe know that you are open to the universal information that is out there for you.

When I come into a home or office, I always look for signs if people are connecting with their inner wisdom and if they are open to mentoring and teachers. If you wish to use the Law of Attraction at its best, then you need to be teachable.

Every successful person I ever met had a spiritual or religious practice or believed in scientific knowledge. Royal families always had priests, advisors, and teachers around them. Great compassionate leaders know the value of wisdom.

Your home needs to show that you are open to the knowledge and wisdom that the Universe can offer you. If you are closing yourself off from the treasures of the Universe, then your home will reflect that too. Are you awake to your inner voice or do you still sleep and have no connection with your Inner Self?

To have wisdom, it is necessary to attract mentors, coaches, and teachers that will share their wisdom with you. You also need time to reflect, to meditate and to contemplate. Creating a space for wisdom is part of what you need to attract. You need to take time to go within, to pray, to do your affirmations, and to have time to listen to your self- improvement audios. You need to take time for seminars, classes and webinars. Wisdom can be found in the words of elders, in books, in dreams and in visions.

Surround Yourself with Wisdom Energy:

- Place a yellow item in the Northeast area of your bedroom, office, or living room to attract more wisdom in your life
- Make a room where you can recharge your energy
- Play meditation music
- Place images of angels, divine mothers such as Mother Mary, Kuan Yin, Buddha, Jesus, or any other divine statue
- Have an inspirational book within reach for when you need it
- Create an altar or a meditation area and have a prayer chair
- Keep self-improvement CDs in your car
- Burn incense
- Light a prayer candle for special requests
- Place crystals or an amethyst in the Northeast section of your living area

- Have a dream journal or Transformation Journal next to your bed

Activate Your Home for Wisdom
In the Northeast of your bedroom, office or living room, place a symbol, a book, or an image that represents wisdom for you.

Activate Your Home for Mentorship
Place in the Northwest of your bedroom or living room a book or picture of your mentor, spiritual, religious advisor, psychologist or coach.

Activate Your Personal Wisdom Direction
In your personal wisdom direction, you can also place the book you are currently reading, a flyer of the seminar you wish to follow or the music that inspires you.

Extra tips:

- Always travel with an inspirational book
- Always have some meditation or inspirational music with you on your technical gadgets
- Never sit with your back to the entrance if you wish to always be the Master of your life

Your Energy Journal

The Diamond Energy Principle of Compassion

"I Am Compassionate for All That Is in the World"

2/ The Diamond Energy Principle of Compassion

Compassion is the twentieth Diamond Energy Principle and activates your knowledge and inspiration. You will learn how to activate this within you and in the space around you to attract 33.3% more wisdom.

a/ Your Inner Activation of Compassion

When you choose to change your life by attracting the right things, people and outcomes, you need to start being compassionate about what you have attracted so far. Don't start judging yourself.

You have based your current life on what you knew before but now you can start transforming yourself and your environment based on the new information you have received. You cannot judge yourself for not knowing.

You can divide your life into two sections: life before knowing the Law of Attraction and after knowing this wisdom. The fact you didn't know it in the past, doesn't make you less important or made life less good. It is just a different life experience.

There is a Zen saying that can help you: "Before Enlightenment, you do the laundry. After Enlightenment, you do the laundry." Life goes on even if you are now enlightened about the Laws of the Universe.

Don't look down on others because they don't know these ideas yet. Indeed, there are people out there who live their lives unconsciously; they are asleep. But you can't judge them for this. Remember not so long ago you were soundly asleep yourself.

Life gets so much easier when you stop judging yourself and others. You lose so much energy by judging and you don't feel great about it in your heart. Today, people love to hear the latest gossip about famous people so that they can talk about them all day. When you walk in their shoes for a mile, perhaps you will speak differently.

Once you really master compassion, you will be treating others with more patience and gentleness, and you will be more open to give others advice when they ask for it. But stay open to yourself and have Compassion for yourself. If you feel you need some advice and support in going to the next level of mastery, the Law of Attraction will help you.

Make sure you are easy on yourself about trying something new that doesn't really work out. There are many approaches to the Law of Attraction, and everyone has a different story to share. Some will work for you and others will not. It is not always about you. It can just be the wrong approach for you.

It is possible you have many excuses about not following your dreams or you blame others or even God. Don't be so hard on yourself. Just be compassionate and let go and start all over. Every day is a new Universe.

In 1998, I travelled with thirty-six students to Nepal to visit the Himalayas and many Tibetan monasteries. It was a challenging journey. I worked with a woman who helped organize this trip. She was Western but she knew the country and the people very well. I found out on the trip that she knew them so well that she had organized extra deals behind my back to fill her pockets.

One day we went to some local artists to buy statues of Buddha. I wanted to give money to the artists directly rather than give money to the shops that take some of the proceeds. I asked everyone to give the price they asked for and not to bargain, as it was still better than in the shops.

After visiting them, she stayed behind in the streets. I was worried and went back to search for her. I found her demanding payment from the artists because she created revenues for them. She already was very well paid for organizing the trip, but she wanted extra cash. I was shocked.

At that moment, a Tibetan monk crossed my path in the street in his red and saffron yellow outfit. He smiled and looked at me and at her, and then he said to me in English: "Buddha is compassionate." At that moment, my whole judgment toward this woman disappeared. Who was I to judge her? Who was I to be shocked? It wasn't my place to judge her.

She showed up later that night, bragging to everyone about the new outfits she just bought with the money that I knew she received underhandedly. I complimented her on her beauty with grace, knowing that my intentions were pure and that she had still to learn her lesson.

Diamond Energy Exercise

Take time to relax and close your eyes. Connect within by breathing consciously in and out. Then visualize yourself in a beautiful space in nature where you feel in complete harmony and peace. Imagine there is a quantum rainbow in the sky with 24 colors. You connect in with the saffron yellow aspect of this rainbow and fill your body and energy field with this color. From your head to your feet, you are filled with the saffron yellow energy of the Universe.

Focus now on your heart chakra in the center of your chest. As you breathe in, think about someone that you wish to be more compassionate with in your family, your friends or in the world. Radiate the saffron yellow color out from your heart chakra while you breathe out. Imagine that a ray of saffron yellow is reaching the heart of the person you are sending it to. You are radiating this color without expectations or judgments.

Say the following affirmation: ***"I Am Compassionate with you."*** Focus again on the beautiful space around you in your visualization and open your eyes.

b/ The Diamond Energy Color of Compassion

The color of compassion is saffron yellow. Saffron yellow is the color used by the Tibetan Buddhist monks in their outfits. Saffron is an herb that is used to harmonize food, and the smell of this herb is a mellow one that calms the nerves. The Tibetan monks and nuns are considered symbols of walking the path of compassion towards all living beings.

They honor life with such compassion that they don't believe in killing any animal for pleasure or food. But they are compassionate to people, who according to their cultures, still do. There is no judgment involved; it is simply a different way of living your life.

How can You Use This Color, Saffron Yellow?

- Paint your bedroom or living room in saffron yellow to create a more compassionate atmosphere, especially if a lot of fighting and bickering is happening in your relationships
- You can start with placing some saffron yellow pillows on the couch where you sit with people who might be judging you
- Place a bouquet of saffron yellow flowers between you and a judgmental colleague
- At the entrance to your home, place a saffron yellow rug with the word "Welcome" on it
- Place a saffron yellow item in the Northeast of the living room or in the bedroom

c/ Your Feng Shui Activation of Compassion

A compassionate person will have no judgment on themselves or on others. Even when you know some Feng Shui tips and you look around people's homes, avoid judging others for their lack of good Feng Shui.

When walking into people's homes and offices I have learned to be compassionate for what people have created in their lives. However, it is important that if you know something is not supporting their lives or their goals, especially towards their children, to insist on making the changes.

Any time I see a child sleeping with images of war or fighting around them, or images with skulls or negative words, I insist to their parents to remove the items and see how their child changes.

Surround Yourself with Compassionate Energy:

- Add images or statues of gods and goddesses that embody compassion in your home
- Place books or movies in your library about saints or people who stand for world peace or compassion, like Nelson Mandela or Martin Luther King Jr.
- Gather items that no longer serve you and bring them to a Goodwill organization near you
- Keep a little bowl of coins that you can share with homeless people
- Remove all judgmental words and sentences, especially around children's rooms. Some children write on their door: "Stay out" so provide them with positive alternatives.
- Place images of harmony around your home
- Remove images of war and conflict
- Place images or statues of elders and native people, in your living space but ensure that they are depicted without weapons

- Place images or statues of different kinds of religions and include books about different beliefs
- Avoid images or statues of dead animals
- Avoid reading gossip magazines

Extra Tips:

- Create soft lighting when it starts getting dark
- When you bathe, put candles around your bath and make sure you have essential oils in your bathwater
- Soft pillows and furniture will create more compassion in your family home

Your Energy Journal

The Diamond Energy Principle of Clarity

"I Am Clarity in All I Am and All I Do"

3/ The Diamond Energy Principle of Clarity

Clarity is the twenty-first Diamond Energy Principle and activates your knowledge and inspiration. You will learn how to activate this within you and in the space around you to attract 33.3% more wisdom.

a/ Inner Activation of Clarity

The Universe is like a shopping center. You can ask for anything. When you walk into a shop and ask for a dress, the owner of the store or the assistant will tell you to look around for what you like and need. You might look around for a few minutes before deciding that they have nothing.

This is not entirely true however; you just were not clear in your request. But if you walk in and you know what you want, say a dress, size 12, in cotton, light blue with white and you tell this to the owner, they will direct you to the right area of the shop. In this way, you will not lose time and you will more likely be able to find the item that works perfectly. You will come out of the shop with a dress, and you will probably tell your friends how happy you are with your shopping experience in that place.

But the shop and the shop owner in both cases are the same. The only thing that changed is that you went in with more clarity about what you wished for.

Without knowledge of what you want, you are not working with the Law of Attraction and it will have no results. You must write your shopping list in detail.

The more details you have, the faster and more accurate the Universe provides. I know I love shopping when I can walk and look around, but only when I have time on my hand. If I need something fast and effortlessly, I ask the Universe for help and I give details because I will be guided in the right way to manifest my desires.

Clarity is something you need to keep vigilant about because your desires may change. Check in regularly to see if what you put out to attract is still up to date. I check it every few weeks. Some long-term ideas will remain the same, but some short-term goals can change. Shop with clarity in the Universal shopping center.

When I want to move into a new home I don't simply wish for a new home in a certain area. I tell the Universe exactly what I'm looking for. What the home needs to look like, in which area, and how many miles from a school and shopping center. How far does the home need to be from the freeway? What is the views outside the house? How much do I want to pay? What kind of neighbors will I have and if they'll have children? Would I like a pool, a hot tub, a garden, etc. Do I want to buy it or rent it?

The more details, the easier it is for the Universe to find a home for my family.

Recall the vision board of John Assaraf in the book "The Secret". The Universe gave him exactly the home he desired, not just one that looked like it. When it comes to communicating with the Universe, more details are better because the Universe can and will provide.

The same happens with relationships. People tell me that they put an image on their vision board of what they want their future husband or wife to look like. They also need to provide details about the kind of person they wish to attract - the kind of personality, interests, goals, etc. that they most relate to. For relationships, I suggest the next set of detailed desires.

Describe in detail the kind of partner you wish to attract physically, emotionally, spiritually, and professionally. From which area will this person come from and where do you want to meet them – in a club or through friends? What values, characteristics, social outlooks, etc. should the person have? Describe in detail what this partner is looking for in you: of course, focus on the good characteristics of yourself that this partner is looking for.

For example: I put out to the Universe that I would like to attract a partner who would be okay with the spiritual and clairvoyant side of me. I forgot to put in as detail that he had to be a good dancer. So that detail unfortunately was not filled. My husband is not a great dancer, but that's okay because he's a great man supporting my vision and my work in the world.

Describe in detail what kind of relationship you wish to have with this partner. For example: whether you want to travel together or join the same church. The Universe reads what we're asking for through images, information, and numbers.

Put no timing into your request, making sure to write it in the present tense instead: Here and Now and give the Universe enough time to make it happen. It is better to be surprised by the speed of the manifestation. If you wish to attract the partner of your dreams in one hour, then you will be disappointed.

For your financial goals, I will always tell people that they need to come up with numbers that are comfortable for them but then add the words "and more" afterwards.

Say how much money you'd like to be making in one year but then add the words "or sooner". What is a good amount? Take an amount that you feel is possible. Then add at least 25% to it. In this way, you stretch your expectations.

For example: Perhaps you'd like to make $2,000 per month in six months or sooner. You can instead ask that you'd like to make $3,000, and then ask for a timeframe of six months to a year. Or ask for more money in more time (like one, three, or ten years). When you put out amounts that are too big right now for your unconscious fears, you will not manifest them. Go step-by-step and feel comfortable with your goals. When it is possible for you the Universe will give you more and sooner.

I had a client who told me that he wanted to be successful in his business. One of the ideas that I shared with him was to put out an image of a sailboat that would sail wealth and success into his life. He said that he had this image hanging exactly across the entrance door of the office. That seemed good, but I asked him to be very sure because the Universe watches for all the details.

He took a closer look and realized that the sailboat was sailing along a river that ended in a waterfall. That is exactly how things were for his business: the opportunities came in, but then they all went downhill!

In another story, a lady received a painting from her lover, six weeks before he left her, a painting of a man on a boat and a lady at the beach.

She wanted to keep the painting because she believed the man would come back. But if you looked at the details of the image, the man was sailing away from the beach. The intention of the lover was already visible in the painting.

As long as she kept the painting up, any man would sail away from her. She changed the picture for a happy couple. She found another man that made her even more happier than her previous partner. Clarity is in the details.

Diamond Energy Exercise

Take time to relax and close your eyes. Connect within by breathing consciously in and out. Then visualize yourself in a beautiful space in nature where you feel in complete harmony and peace. Imagine there is a quantum rainbow in the sky with 24 colors. You connect in with the aqua blue aspect of this rainbow and fill your body and energy field with this color.

From your head to your feet, you are filled with the aqua blue energy of the Universe. As you breathe in, you fill yourself with clarity and as you breathe out you are letting go of every thought, feeling and past action that limited your inner clarity.

After this you can connect with a situation, a goal or a relationship where you wish to have more inner clarity in and visualize the color aqua blue around and in it, until you feel it is completely clear.

Say the following affirmation: ***"I Am Clarity in All I Am and in All I Do."*** Focus again on the beautiful space around you in your visualization and open your eyes.

b/ The Diamond Energy Color of Clarity

The color of clarity is aqua blue. Have you ever been on a holiday to a tropical island where the water is so clear you can see the fish swim in it? "Aqua" is the Latin word for "water", and water should always be clear. Likewise, the Universe should always be able to understand your messages clearly.

How Can You Use This Color, Aqua Blue?

- You can place an aqua blue item at the entrance so that clarity lives in the household
- Place an aqua blue item on your desk or wear something in this color when you need to set your goals or do brainstorming
- Make sure you place a bubbling fountain in the North area of your office or living room to attract clear insights into your future. Place it in the Southeast area of your office or living room if you wish for clarity in your finances

c/ Your Feng Shui Activation of Clarity

The Universe reads your home and everything that is your home. Your home is a constant message to the Universe. I am sure by reading this book, that you have already changed the images and colors in your home. It is now a good time to look over everything you placed and all the changes you have made.

Double check that what you put out is what you wish for. Is it detailed enough, and is it what you really desire?

Surround Yourself with Clarity:

- Place an aqua blue item in the North area of your office
- Add your logo to your office to clearly indicate what business is residing in this particular place
- Display images that show what you desire
- Display products or images of your products in your company
- Clean your aquariums, fountains, and still water features
- Direct the flow of Chi in your hallways by hanging mirrors or paintings
- Indicate where people need to go with maps or signs

- When the staircase is across from the front door, place a plant next to the staircase so the energy does not rush up
- Use lights in your garden to enhance the beauty of your home and to make the area safer at night

Extra Tips:

- Make sure your windows are clean because they represent the eyes of your home
- Clean your mirrors because they are symbols of clarity

Your Energy Journal

The Diamond Energy Principle of Focus

"I Focus on What is Important in the World"

4/ The Diamond Energy Principle of Focus

Focus is the twenty-second Diamond Energy Principle and activates your knowledge and inspiration. You will learn how to activate this within you and in the space around you to attract 33.3% more wisdom.

a/ Your Inner Activation of Focus

In order to make the Law of Attraction work for you, you need to focus for a while on what it is you wish to receive from the Universe. By focusing, you put the energy in flow. Everything you give attention to, will manifest. Focus is a positive way of giving attention.

Focusing is not an emotional way of giving attention; rather it is a mindful way of telling the Universe what you want. Mindfulness is more like giving a goal attention by thinking about it with your objective mind and by visualizing how it will feel when it does manifest.

You know that it will happen, easily and effortlessly, because it is the Law of the Universe. It always happens at the right time. And when it doesn't happen, there is something you need to learn before it can happen, or someone or something needs to be in place beforehand.

Focusing is more than just concentrating. It is also creating an atmosphere around you that represents what you desire. When you wish for harmony, then you need to listen to harmonious sounds and not create conflicts or keep judging yourself and others. If you wish for beauty; then you can start by making yourself beautiful. Use anything you have to confirm what you really desire.

The information you receive in this book about how to implement your wishes in your Outer Universe is a great way of focusing. By sitting in another direction, you will focus differently on the world.

Often people tell me that they started having a new perspective on their problems because they were sitting or sleeping in a different position.

You now have a different focus on the world. If you are still sitting with your back to the door, why don't you try turning your desk around to see how differently your focus is?

Diamond Energy Exercise

Take time to relax and close your eyes. Connect within by breathing consciously in and out. Then visualize yourself in a beautiful space in nature where you feel in complete harmony and peace. Imagine there is a quantum rainbow in the sky with 24 colors. You connect in with the iris blue aspect of this rainbow and fill your body and energy field with this color. From your head to your feet, you are filled with the iris blue energy of the Universe.

Focus now on your heart chakra in the center of your chest. As you breathe in, think about someone that you wish positive focus for in your family, your friends or in the world. Radiate the iris blue color out from your heart chakra while you breathe out. Imagine that a ray of iris blue is reaching the heart of the person you are sending it to. You are radiating this color without expectations or judgments.

Say the following affirmation: ***"I Create Focus for you."*** Focus again on the beautiful space around you in your visualization and open your eyes.

b/ The Diamond Energy Color of Focus

The color of focus is iris blue. The symbol of the French kings was the Iris flower: the fleur-de-lis. The most well-known king to use that symbol was Louis XIV who was very focused on his goals. So focused, in fact, that he proclaimed, "I am the government."

Interestingly he introduced Feng Shui to the Western courts. His palace was the ideal Feng Shui for his success as a king.

How Can You Use This Color, Iris Blue?

- Place projects you need to focus on in folders that are in this color or have the name of the project on it in iris blue
- When you have a long day ahead in the office, wear something iris blue so that your focus will be sharp.
- In the conference room, place some iris blue items at the meeting so that everyone will be focused on a positive outcome and create the results they desire.

c/ Your Feng Shui Activation of Focus

My experience is that certain aspects of a home can really create concentration problems. Like sleeping and working under wooden beams, having sharp objects pointed at you like a bow and arrow. Even having different kinds of music playing at the same time or having several doors leading into one room can lead to lack of focus.

Surround Yourself with Focused Energy:

- Place an image of an iris blue flower, or any item in this color, in the East area of your office
- Choose interior colors that match and don't clash
- Cover any beams you have been sleeping under with a white fabric in the color of the ceiling or have a canopy bed, and cover any beam you sit under whilst working
- Keep the master bathroom door closed
- Hang a convex Pakua mirror above the frame of your outside door to reflect the sharp edge of your neighbor's home and any sharp object pointed at your house
- Make sure that all the books on the shelves of bookcases are flush with the edge of the shelf because an exposed edge disturbs the people sitting close to it

- Always declutter your desk and workspace before the end of your day

Extra tips:

- Remove plants with sharp points, like yuccas, cactus, and palm trees
- When you have a window behind your bed, hang heavy curtains or place a screen so that the moonlight doesn't distract you from a good night's sleep

Your Energy Journal

The Diamond Energy Principle of Transformation

"I Am Transformation in All I Am and All I Do"

5/ The Diamond Energy Principle of Transformation.

Transformation is the twenty-third Diamond Energy Principle and activates your knowledge and inspiration. You will learn how to activate this within you and in the space around you to attract 33.3% more wisdom.

a/ Your Inner Activation of Transformation

Using the Law of Attraction is a transformational approach for many of you and this book offers a more expanded view on it. I have seen how it changes people's lives when they transform their environments as well. Both your conscious and unconscious brain power will be activated.

When you start using the Law of Attraction, you need to keep records of your activations, cures and results. I suggest keeping a Diamond Energy Journal to track when you made the changes and when you saw the transformations start to happen. Luckily, I have created one for you; check out my website:
www.MarieDiamond.com.

Most of the time changes will happen within nine days, nine weeks or nine months. You have sent a message out using signals that are constantly processing. The Universe then finds a way to manifest your message into your life.

Sometimes people around you experience the changes in you faster than you notice them. They will tell you that you have changed and may ask what you've done. Or they'll tell you that you look more relaxed.

But transformation sometimes happens when you start feeling like what you have been doing so far is no longer working and you will make decisions when you get inspired to live differently.

Ultimately, though, transformation can only happen if you take action. The sooner you incorporate some of my tips, the faster you will get results and can begin realizing the life of your dreams. Try these changes for at least nine weeks, even if you don't like the changes immediately. Let the Universe reveal to you what changes your environment can inspire.

In order to transform your life, you will need to step out of your comfort zone. The moment you ask for changes, your mind will start creating insights from different angles. CH+ANGE = CHI+ANGLE.

Even if you don't want changes, just reading this book will give you new insights. From new insights, change and transformation will start happening. Some clients tell me that the moment they connected with me by sending an email, their lives started changing. They told me that I brought them good luck. Well perhaps I did, but just by them taking action, they told the Universe they wanted to transform their life and transformation started happening.

When I was in my late thirties, I had a large group of students in my home country Belgium. The people were very dedicated to studying with me. I had started to go back and forth between Belgium and the USA to pursue my dreams to reach millions of people with my message. I was torn between what I had created in Europe and what I was creating in the USA.

One day I visited a young Rinpoche in Nepal: A Lama of high rank. He was only four years old and he placed an opal shawl around my neck while looking in my eyes and blessing me. After that meeting, I had a powerful dream that told me I didn't have to choose and that, if I focused on the world at large, both continents would be part of my journey.

A huge relief came over me because I felt responsible for the ones I helped on their journey. Now I could let go and know that everyone was responsible for their own journey. The only thing I could do was share how they could transform, but I didn't have to carry the responsibility of their journeys. New freedom gave me the opening to move to the USA and know that my old students would be totally fine. I was part of their transformational journey and they could stay connected with me in the future if they wanted to. It was their choice, not mine.

Diamond Energy Exercise

Take time to relax and close your eyes. Connect within by breathing consciously in and out. Then visualize yourself that you are in a beautiful space in nature where you feel in complete harmony and peace. Imagine there is a quantum rainbow in the sky with 24 colors. You connect in with the opal aspect of this rainbow and fill your body and energy field with this color.

From your head to your feet, you are filled with the opal energy of the Universe. As you breathe in, you fill yourself with transformation and as you breathe out you are letting go of every thought, feeling and past action that limited your inner transformation.

After this you can connect with a situation, a goal or a relationship where you wish to have more inner transformation about and visualize the color opal around and in it, until you feel it is completely transformed.

Say the following affirmation: ***"I Am Transformation in All I Am and in All I Do."*** Focus again on the beautiful space around you in your visualization and open your eyes.

b/ The Diamond Energy Color of Transformation

The color of transformation is opal. The opal is a stone that, in the sunlight, reflects the colors of the rainbow. It reflects the colors blue, yellow, rose, white, green, ruby red, violet, peach, aqua, magenta, and gold.

The legends say that the opal stone can only be worn by strong women and Divine Mothers. It is definitely a very feminine energy, but anyone can use this color. It will help you bring your creative ideas to manifestation.

How Can You Use This Color, Opal?

- Place opal-colored candles in front of a picture of someone whose relationship you have with, you wish you transform
- Wear opal shawls or shirts when you have an important meeting that could transform your career

c/ Your Feng Shui Activation of Transformation.

Transformation is constantly happening in your life. One of the basic books that Feng Shui is based on is the "Book of Changes", also called "I Ching." Life is a constant stream of changes, but many people have fallen asleep in their lives and haven't transformed at all. They are still living in the same environment, they still have the same habits, and they still visit the same pub.

Transformation is about having the courage to make a difference in your life. Changing your home is a great step. Changing the pictures and the wallpaper that has been hanging up for the last thirty years is not only a visible step of change, but is also an internal change. Shifts of energy can only happen when you open yourself to something transformational.

It is easier to shift something outside of yourself than it is to shift a pattern in your life. But eventually your Inner Energy will start changing too.

Surround Yourself with Transformational Energy:

- Place an opal or an opalescent item in the Northwest of your living room
- Complete little jobs around the home or office that you have been avoiding
- Spend more time with your children or with friends
- Express your feelings more by communicating or by doing artwork
- Pay attention to the people around you that encourage you to pursue your dreams. Open yourself to find the right resources
- Realize that your friends can help you find your ideal partner
- Allow your marriage to become more romantic
- Watch your cash flow improve and make investments better and stronger

Extra Tips:

- Do not try to be a perfectionist. There is no such thing as perfect Feng Shui. Wind and water always change and energy always flows. What is perfect today may not be perfect tomorrow
- What you wish to attract today is different from what you wish to attract tomorrow. There is no problem in this. Change your wish and change your environment and the Universe will react the same way: it will bring you what you wish for

Your Energy Journal

The Diamond Energy Principle of Faith

"I Have Faith in All That is in the World"

6/ The Diamond Energy Principle of Faith

Faith is the twenty-fourth Diamond Energy Principle and activates your knowledge and inspiration. You will learn how to activate this within you and in the space around you to attract 33.3% more wisdom.

a/ Your Inner Activation of Faith

In order to create results in your life with the Laws of Attraction you don't need to believe them. They are working no matter what. The Law of Attraction is not a religion. Many great spiritual and religious leaders and philosophers have mentioned it, but you don't have to believe in it in order for it to work.

Even if you reject the existence of this, it will work. Most people experience that what they fear the most is what happens because they attract what they put out there.

When you start working with the Law of Attraction, the results can seem magical. It is, after all, a metaphysical Law that works beyond the physical world of cause and effect. It works on the energetic level of your life. The only thing you need to have is faith in what you place around you and whether it is what you really want.

Feeling confidence in yourself is always a plus point. If you don't know what you really wish for in detail, then hang something that is more neutral.

If you like to have peace in your family; you can hang an image of world peace. It is more general, but it will send out the right message. Your family is part of the world. The more detailed and the more focused your request is the better the results and the faster it is.

Faith is having confidence that God/ the Universe is hearing your message and is taking care of you. Once you have shared the message with the Universe, don't resist the change and have faith that the Universe knows exactly how to bring your request to your life.

Your faith needs to rest in the fact that the Law of Attraction works, it does regardless if you believe in it or not. Many people still ask me, "but how?" and I have to tell them that I don't know the How, only God knows. Have faith that God/the Universe works in ways beyond your imagination.

In 1994, I shared with my students in Belgium that I would bring the 24 Diamond Energy Principles to the world, and that people in the USA and across the world would do the Tubes of Light meditation. I remember specifically that some of my students came to me and asked if I was not arrogant to think that a thirty-one year-old woman from Belgium would be able to do this.

After my near-death experience when I was fifteen and since my enlightenment experience at twenty-six, my faith has been stronger than a diamond. The Universe knows all, and it will be fulfilled as I ask. Perhaps faith can look like arrogance, but it isn't. Knowing deep inside you that the Universe will provide shows a deep faith in the Universal Laws.

My spiritual Master shared with me that I am a diamond and that I hold this vibration for the world. No wonder, since I was fourteen years of age, I have listened to Neil Diamond, and that I attracted a husband who, since he was fourteen years old too, is a very big Neil Diamond fan. This is one of the precious things we have in common. My husband suggested I use this spiritual name given by my Master when coming to the USA, and since then it has brought me good luck. Does having faith mean you are confident all the time? No, it doesn't. Does faith mean that you are never in doubt or in fear? No, it doesn't.

But you are more able to redirect that doubt and fear towards positive vibrations because of your faith in a higher knowledge.

When you really have faith, start acting upon what you wish to accomplish. The first action step you need to take is to change the environment around you. Tell the Universe, "Yes, I have faith that I will be more powerful, therefore I will change my desk around." Or "Yes, I have faith that I will make more money, therefore I will buy myself this little fountain and put it in the right direction."

Looking at how my life unfolded, I can really tell you that by using what I share with you in this book, I have received more faith and confidence in acting faster when the Universe offered me an insight or a solution.

As I changed the environment around me, I felt more confident that what I wished for could become true because I saw the visual outside of me, and I felt the vibration of change around me.

The Law of Attraction is happening inside of you and in the Universal fields, but you don't see anything change until it manifests. Without using this knowledge, I would never have had the Faith to leave Belgium and move to the US.

One morning I woke up on my visit to California and I knew that on that day, I would find my home in San Francisco. I did, and I called my husband and told him to start packing because we would be moving in three weeks. So, we did.

Results That Will Show Up When You Have Faith:

- You recognize great results with this book and share them with your friends
- You feel that you have more patience with yourself and what you wish to accomplish

- You feel more grateful for what you have created so far, and you know that you will receive more things to be grateful for
- You have overcome your resistance to change
- You see the Universe giving you results, and you enjoy the process of the Law of Attraction

Diamond Energy Exercise

Take time to relax and close your eyes. Connect within by breathing consciously in and out. Then visualize yourself in a beautiful space in nature where you feel in complete harmony and peace. Imagine there is a quantum rainbow in the sky with 24 colors. You connect in with the diamond aspect of this rainbow and fill your body and energy field with this color. From your head to your feet, you are filled with the diamond energy of the Universe.

Focus now on your heart chakra in the center of your chest. As you breathe in, think about someone that you wish to have faith in, for your family, your friends or in the world. Radiate the diamond color out from your heart chakra while you breathe out. Imagine that a ray of diamond is reaching the heart of the person you are sending it to. You are radiating this color without expectations or judgments.

Say the following affirmation: ***"I have Faith in You."*** Focus again on the beautiful space around you in your visualization and open your eyes.

b/ The Diamond Energy Color of Faith

The color of faith is diamond colored. Diamonds are forever. Ladies who wear diamonds tend to feel more confident. When you receive a Diamond ring from your boyfriend, you feel more confident that you two will make it to the altar and through life with each other.

Some men have told me that when they offered a diamond ring to their partners, it was because they decided that they were the one for him. It is seen as the ultimate gemstone and it holds great power. This power of faith or confidence will encourage you to let the Universe take care of you and your wishes.

I was living in the USA for a couple of years and I was going through a tough time. I was struggling financially. A student of mine sent me a small envelope with a diamond ring inside. It was gorgeous. I called her, not sure what to say and even doubting that she would actually send me a real diamond ring. She said on the phone: "It is a diamond ring with a value of $10,000." I was shocked, how did she have the faith by mail in an envelope, without being stolen? She said: "I have been practicing the Diamond Energy Principle of faith after doing your seminar. I felt you needed a little bit of faith too. So, I sent you this ring, as a token of my appreciation. You changed my life around. After your Feng Shui consultation and your Inner Diamond meditation seminar, I met the love of my life and I was healed."

I never had a diamond ring before and I never received or made $10,000 in one day. I started wearing it and it has brought me more financial luck. The month afterwards I was paid $10,000 for a one-day consultation for a company and my financial life changed.

Even if you feel that the Law of Attraction is not working immediately, keep going. Ultimately, the most beautiful energy is release. Know that, today, millions of people are opening themselves to this wisdom with remarkable results.

How Can You Use This Color Diamond?

- Place quartz crystals in your children's bedrooms if they lack faith in themselves
- Buy glass or diamond-shaped items and place them on your desk to stimulate confidence in your work or product

c/ Your Feng Shui Activation of Faith

Some people don't feel as strong and confident as they should when they enter their office. It is hard for them to create a field of harmony in the place where they make a great field of manifesting. Others may feel great at work, but the moment they enter their home they feel weak and are unable to concentrate.

It is important to place your images when you need confidence. Or even put out books about self-esteem or confidence, or images of people that have Faith in the Universe/God.

Surround Yourself with Faith Energy:

- Place a diamond-shaped stone in the Northwest of your bedroom to stimulate faithfulness in your relationship
- Place pictures around you with great teachers and mentors who have believed in you and who have tremendous faith in the Law of Attraction
- Display quotes of people who believed in themselves and attained their goals
- Place an image of a diamond-shaped crystal

Extra Tips:

- Hang crystal balls at your window so that the sun can shine on them and create rainbows. It will create a feeling that the Universe is taking care of you
- Also celebrate every great result that manifests with a little bouquet of flowers, a little dinner party, or a high five with your partner. The more you enjoy the results, the greater results the Universe will send you

Your Energy Journal

What Are the Next Steps After Reading This Book?

When I was studying piano as a child, I once asked my teacher: "I can read the music and I understand the music, now what?" He said: "Practice the music and enjoy it."

My suggestion will be "practice" the steps I suggested to you and enjoy each step in manifesting your goals. Some of you will read this book one time and others will see it as their go-to book for changing their life. You can ask a question and open up the book spontaneously and get the right answer. Let this book be a good friend on your Diamond Energy Journey and share it with others.

Step 1: Get your Free Energy Report

You can visit my website www.MarieDiamond.com and sign up for your Free Energy Report. You will then receive access to your Free Energy report and get your personal directions for Success.

Step 2: Download the Free Marie Diamond App

You can get your Energy Number and your four best directions with the Diamond Compass, your Tubes of Light Meditation, daily messages, and several exclusive free videos. You can also join the Diamond Energy Journey in the premium version with extra videos, affirmations, personal and world meditations, and Feng Shui Tips catered specifically to your Personal Energy Number.

Step 3: Keep the Book Close to You.

Each time you move to another place or start working in another office, make sure that this book is accessible. Each time a friend or a family member has some issues in success, health, relationships or wisdom, you can take this book and share some tips for activating their life and making their reality show of life successful.

Step 4: Share the Results with Others

The next step after practicing and enjoying the music is to share it with others. Share the changes that you made to your home and the results that occurred in your life with others. Sharing creates even more joy and happiness because others will be inspired to start their Transformation. Buy this book as a gift for others and you will help your friends and family transform their own lives.

Step 5: Follow Marie Diamond on Social Media

- Instagram: @Mariediamond8
- TikTok: @ Mariediamond8
- Facebook English Fans & Students: @MarieDiamondFans
- Twitter: @mariediamond888
- Pinterest: @MarieDiamond
- LinkedIn: @MarieDiamond
- Clubhouse: @Mariediamond
- Podcast: The Marie Diamond Podcast

AUTHOR

Marie Diamond is a globally renowned Transformational Leader and star of the worldwide phenomenon "The Secret". She uses her extraordinary knowledge of quantum physics, the Law of Attraction, and Feng Shui to help people transform their environments and their lives. Her vision is to enlighten more than 500 million people during her lifetime.

Her clients include A-list celebrities in film and music (including Steven Spielberg, Big Sean, Jason Bateman and Jodie Foster) and top-selling authors and speakers such as Rhonda Byrne, Jack Canfield, John Gray, the late Bob Proctor, Marianne Williamson and Vishen Lakhiani. She also advises leaders from Fortune 500 companies, sports athletes, governments, and royal families. Marie Diamond combines her intuitive gifts, the growing science of energy flow, ancient wisdom, and modern tools to enlighten homes, businesses, and people. She is known for her passion to help create enlightened leaders around the world.

She is a founding member of the Transformational Leadership Council, created by Jack Canfield, and President of the Association of Transformational Leaders in Europe.

She has more than one million online and in-person students in more than 190 countries. You can connect with her for personal mentoring, consultations, seminars, online courses, eBooks, and home study courses at www.MarieDiamond.com. Her Spanish students can join her at www.MarieDiamondespanol.com.

Her teachings are published in online programs such as Mind Valley, Learning Strategies and YouUnity. For her charity work, she is a knighted Dame.

Currently, she lives between the south of France, London and the USA with her family and her dogs.

Made in the USA
Coppell, TX
21 February 2023

13223404R00134